REMEMBERING THE KANJI 3

BY THE SAME AUTHOR

Remembering the Kana: A Guide to Reading and Writing the Japanese Syllabaries in 3 Hours Each. Honolulu: University of Hawai'i Press, 2007 (1987)

Remembering the Kanji 1: A Complete Course on How Not to Forget the Meaning and Writing of Japanese Characters. Honolulu: University of Hawai'i Press, 2007 (1977)

Remembering the Kanji 2: A Systematic Guide to Reading Japanese Characters. Honolulu: University of Hawai'i Press, 2008 (1987)

Kanji para recordar I: Curso mnemotécnico para el aprendizaje de la escritura y el significado de los caracteres japoneses (with Marc Bernabé and Verònica Calafell). Barcelona: Herder Editorial, 2005 (2001)

Kanji para recordar II: Guía sistemática para la lectura de los caracteres japoneses (with Marc Bernabé and Verònica Calafell). Barcelona: Herder Editorial, 2004

Kana para recordar: Curso mnemotécnico para el aprendizaje de los silabarios japoneses (with Marc Bernabé and Verònica Calafell). Barcelona: Herder Editorial, 2005 (2003)

Die Kanji lernen und behalten 1. Bedeutung und Schreibweise der japanischen Schriftzeichen (with Robert Rauther). Frankfurt am Main: Vittorio Klostermann Verlag, 2006 (2005)

Die Kanji lernen und behalten 2. Systematische Anleitung zu den Lesungen der japanischen Schriftzeichen (with Robert Rauther). Frankfurt am Main: Vittorio Klostermann Verlag, 2006

Die Kana lernen und behalten. Die japanische Silbenschrift lesen und schreiben in je drei Stunden (with Klaus Gresbrand). Frankfurt am Main: Vittorio Klostermann Verlag, 2006

Kanji: Imaginar para aprender (with Rafael Shoji). São Paulo: JBC Editora, 2007

REMEMBERING THE KANJI

VOL. 3

*Writing and Reading Japanese Characters
for Upper-Level Proficiency*

James W. Heisig
&
Tanya Sienko

SECOND EDITION

University of Hawai'i Press
HONOLULU

First edition: 2nd printing, 1995
Second edition: 1st printing, 2008

12 11 10 09 08 07   6 5 4 3 2 1

Library of Congress Cataloging-in-Publication Data

Heisig, James W., 1944-
    Remembering the kanji : a complete course on how not to forget the meaning
    and writing of Japanese characters / James W. Heisig. — 5th ed.
    v. <1> ; cm.
    Includes indexes.
    ISBN 978-0-8248-3165-3 (pbk. : alk. paper)
    1. Japanese language—Orthography and spelling. 2. Chinese characters—
    Japan. 3. Japanese language—Textbooks for foreign speakers—English. I. Title.
PL547.H4 2007
495.6'82421—dc22

                                              2006103109

The typesetting for this book was done at the Nanzan Institute for Religion and Culture.

Contents

INDEXES

Preface

Tanya Sienko

WHEN I FIRST contacted Dr. Heisig with a proposal to add a third volume to *Remembering the Kanji*, I somehow left the impression that it was my rather esoteric needs as a scientist that left me hankering for more kanji than the 2,042 I had learned with his method. Actually, it was not the technical prose of Yukawa and Tomonaga on field theory that were causing me my biggest headaches but ordinary Japanese novels. Having read mystery novels to polish my reading in other languages, I was disappointed to find that the "essential" or "general-use" characters were simply not enough to gain entry into the Japanese thriller. After just a few chapters, my maiden voyage ended on the rocks. So much for "basic literacy," I thought to myself. And so was born the idea for this book.

During the time of the American Occupation, the Japanese writing system underwent a complete overhaul, which saw the number of Chinese characters to be learned during the years of compulsory education reduced to a bare minimum of 1,850. The idea was to simplify the system and facilitate literacy by removing rarely used kanji from circulation. What the reformers did not count on in their long-range plan was the resistance of the general public to the disappearance of many kanji customarily used for names. Families reacted by continuing to name their children with "traditional" names, but the government refused to register the kanji. This resulted in the bizarre situation where a number of Japanese were growing up legally nameless. In 1951 the Ministry of Education grudgingly backed down and approved another 92 "legal" characters for names, followed by another 28 in 1976. In 1981 the number of "general-use" kanji was increased in 1,945 and in 1990 the kanji approved for use in names was increased to 284. This is the situation at present.

Of course, there were still numerous kanji outside the list that continued to be used in place names, or that appeared in books published before the educational reforms and were impractical to update. Over the past twenty years many of these exiled characters have migrated back into daily use. Advertisers often prefer the compactness and precision of older kanji to their phonetic

1

equivalents. Increasing competition has induced universities to include more and more "unofficial" kanji in their entrance examinations. And popular novelists, as always, cling tenaciously to their cache of little-known glyphs as a mark of the trade. Finally, the ubiquitous word processor has turned the distinction between what is "allowed" and what is "disallowed" into something of an anachronism.

For the foreign student who has landed in this mess, there have been only two alternatives: either you adhere to the official list, or you stumble about blindly trying to improve your knowledge as best you can. The idea behind the present book was to offer a third choice: supplementary kanji to lay a solid basis for contemporary Japanese.

In addition to the method of selection explained in Dr. Heisig's introduction, I myself checked the final list against Edward Daub et al., *Comprehending Technical Japanese* (University of Wisconsin Press, 1975), which used frequency lists to determine the 500 kanji most used in technical writings. With the exception of characters specific to one field, this list is represented in the pages that follow.

Of the many people who assisted me in this project, I would like particularly to express my thanks to Ronald D. Mabbitt for help in the cross-referencing and for his many useful suggestions on the structure of the book; and Kanda Yumiko 神田由美子 for checking some of the more obscure compounds.

Introduction

THE AMERICAN PHILOSOPHER William James once wrote that a great idea goes through three stages on its way to acceptance. First, it is dismissed as nonsense. Then it is acknowledged as true, but insignificant. Finally, it is seen to be important, but not really anything new. Time and again history confirms the wisdom of James's observation, but it also reminds us that the very same bias that resists the invasion of novelty also serves to swat away many a flea-brained idea buzzing about for attention.

In this connection, I must admit I am of two minds about *Remembering the Kanji* and its companion volumes. I have always had the sense that there was something flea-brained about the whole project. Its reception by students of the Japanese language across the world has been as much a surprise to me as to the original publishers. We had expected no more than a short buzz, followed by a firm whack into oblivion. From the start I was convinced that if there was anything important in the method, it surely was nothing new. All I had done, after all, was to put some semblance of order into what students of the kanji had always done: trick their minds into making easily forgettable shapes more memorable. The sales of the books, as well as scores of letters from readers, has convinced me that this is, in fact, the case.

On the one hand, the method seems to have proved itself a natural one suited to large numbers of students motivated to study the kanji on their own. On the other, it remains virtually useless for classroom instruction. This is hardly surprising, since it aims to do something the classroom cannot do, namely to tap the imagination of the individual at the individual's own learning pace. To the native speaker of Japanese trained in the traditional school system and trying to teach the Japanese writing system to those whose primary education was outside of the "kanji curtain," it can only appear a distracting gimmick. For one who does not know from experience the question behind the method, the answer—even if it works—makes no sense. Whatever the merits of *Remembering the Kanji* as a *learning* tool, then, its demerits as a *teaching* tool are beyond redemption. This is probably for the best. To force the expectations of the textbook on the method would probably only end up frustrating everyone—teachers and students. The saving grace of the books is that they are simply too flea-brained to run the circuit of "course work."

Letters from readers have combined expressions of gratitude with more good ideas for improvements than I could ever assimilate into subsequent editions. The misprints that had slipped in along the way, thanks again to alert readers, have been periodically corrected in later printings. For the rest I have let the books stand as they are, reckoning that their unpolished edges encourage the very kind of participation that makes them work in the first place.

The one most common request that has haunted me over the years has been for a supplementary volume that would pick up some of the more useful kanji outside the lists propagated as standard by Japan's Ministry of Education. The request always seemed reasonable enough. When I myself had worked through the official list of kanji, I was left with much the same feeling: learning to write the characters is so simple—now if there were some list that could guide me into learning *more* of them.... The only solution I could see was to learn new characters as they showed up in reading. Unfortunately, I kept no records, and could only reply to readers that they, too, let their particular reading habits guide their acquisition of new kanji. But I always knew it was not quite the right answer to an important question.

Then, about a year and a half ago, Tanya Sienko, a theoretical physicist from the United States employed at Japan's National Institute of Science and Technology Policy, persuaded me that something concrete could be done. Her idea was for a volume that would aim at raising proficiency to the level of 3,000 kanji, based on the methods of VOLS. 1 and 2 of *Remembering the Kanji*. The present book is the result of our combined efforts.

The initial decision to aim at a list of 3,000 characters was not based on any established measure of "upper-level proficiency," but simply out of the need for some parameters within which to begin working. As the selecting of new characters progressed, the decision justified itself and was left to stand.

The choice of which kanji to include and which to leave out was far from simple. In 1990 the Ministry of Education published a revised list of characters for use in names, 284 in all. Kanji from this list that had not been covered in VOLS. 1 and 2 were added first, together with all their readings.

The next step was to consult a list of 3,505 characters published in 1963 by the National Japanese Language Research Institute. Since 1956 the Institute had been issuing periodic reports of research on the frequency with which kanji appeared in various fields of study. Based on some 90 academic and popular journals, a team of scholars turned up 3,328 characters, to which the Institute added another 177.[1] Although the list was not based on the Ministry of Education's list of general-use kanji (常用漢字), it includes all the kanji found in the latter (latest revision, 1977) but, as you might suspect, does not include all the

---

[1] 「現代雑誌九十種の用語用字」『国立国語研究所報告』22 (1963).

characters from the Ministry's 1990 revised list for use in names. In any case, all new kanji in the list with a frequency of more than 9 were selected. The following chart shows the breakdown of the frequency and the overlay of kanji used for names. The darkened areas represent the first two groups of kanji checked for inclusion in the present volume:

The next problem was how to sift through the remaining kanji to reach a total of 3,000. The solution consisted in overlaying a completely new system of classification that has taken the world of Chinese characters by storm since the time of the frequency studies.

1978 marks a watershed in the story of the kanji and in the compilation of frequency lists. It was in that year that the Japanese writing system was converted into computer code, opening the way to the use of the personal computer in Japan. There was never any question that Japan would march enthusiastically to the drum of the computer revolution. But to do so, some way had first to be found around the obvious impossibility of squeezing the Japanese writing system into the 7-bit character codes that make up the American Standard Code for Information Interchange (ASCII) character sets. In response to the challenge, the Japan Industrial Standard or JIS was born.

From the outset the JIS classification has never wanted for critics, but the complaints were largely muffled by the sheer thrill of having a simple tool to manipulate the Chinese characters. In the early stages an initial list of less than 3,000 kanji (JIS-1)[2] was installed as standard in personal computers and printers, while a second list of over 4,000 kanji (JIS-2) was sold separately. Writers and specialists grumbled about characters left out of JIS-1 and relegated to the "second-class" status of JIS-2. By the end of the 1980s, both character sets had been adjusted and are now installed as standard in computer equipment.[3]

The kanji that had been left out of both lists were another matter. Nearly all word-processing programs have included utilities for creating 外字 or "excluded characters." Eventually a third set, the JIS-supplement, was devised. To date, it covers an additional 5,801 kanji. This supplement is not yet standard in personal computers and printers, though newer dictionaries include the code numbers that have been assigned.[4] In the near future it is reasonable to expect that they, too, will become standard equipment.

---

[2] JIS-1 includes basic Roman, Greek, and Cyrillic characters, as well as a handful of general-use typesetting symbols.

[3] Meantime, the early 1990s saw the arrival of Unicode, a workable worldwide standard, based on 16-bit code, that would cover all writing and symbol systems. By that time the Japanese JIS had already become a permanent fixture, and adjustments were made to assign it a place in the Unicode structure that would not conflict with Korean and Chinese.

[4] For an example of the most up-to-date kanji dictionary, which was relied on heavily for the production of this book, see: 鎌田正・米山寅太郎著『大漢語林』(Tokyo: Taishūkan, 1992).

The control of language, which has been an important cultural weapon in the arsenal of modern governments for the past four centuries and more, has brought political complications to the computerization of the kanji in Japan, often masquerading in the robes of scholarly objectivity. Indeed, the more voracious the popular appetite for computer access to kanji becomes, the more these issues come to the fore. The Ministry of Education, for example, which seems to have felt slighted by the designers of the new computer standards, still makes no mention of the JIS's existence in its official lists of general-use characters. Meantime, efforts by the Ministry to regulate the number of kanji in general use have been undercut by the very computers it uses to compose and print its regulations. There is no reason to think that the situation will change in the years to come.[5]

Most important for our purposes here, the wealth of characters seems to have retarded research into standards of "upper-level proficiency." After its latest revision in 1990, the tripartite JIS list now contains a whopping 12,156 characters but does nothing to address the problem of frequency of use.

A simple, if time-consuming, procedure was followed in making the selection of the remaining characters for this volume. First, all kanji that appeared less than 9 times in the National Japanese Language Research Institute list *and* which also appeared in JIS-1 were included. The selection was then rounded off with a few characters that fell outside these borders but which, from personal judgment, we thought it best to include. Graphically, the final results look like this:

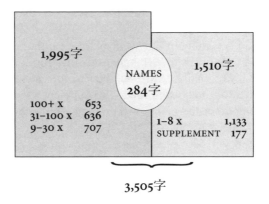

1,995字	NAMES **284**字	**1,510**字
100+ X 653		
31–100 X 636		
9–30 X 707	1–8 X 1,133	
	SUPPLEMENT 177	

3,505字

---

[5] For a fuller account of these conflicts, see special issues of 『しにか』 dealing with 漢字とコンピュータ [Kanji and the computer], 1/2 (1990), and いま漢字の規格化を問う [Rethinking the standardization of the kanji at present], 4/2 (1993).

Chapter 14 reflects the authors' dissatisfaction with the unavoidable arbitrariness in the selection process. It opens with a list of 7 kanji (3001–3007) deliberately excluded from the selection process: 5 of them from the list of names and 2 from JIS-2 that seem worth learning. Space is left for you to record additional characters that you wish to add to the list of "upper-level proficiency" kanji. In future editions, we hope to be able to add to this list of 7, but that will depend on significant numbers of readers sending in their lists for us to compare.

There are six indexes at the end of the volume. Index I shows hand-drawn examples of all the new kanji introduced in this book. Index II is a cumulative listing of all the primitive elements and signal elements introduced in VOLS. 1, 2, and 3. Index III arranges all the kanji from all 3 volumes in order of strokes. Indexes IV and V contain cumulative lists of all the Chinese (*on*) and Japanese (*kun*) readings for all the kanji treated in all 3 volumes. Finally, Index VI is a comprehensive list of all the key words and primitive meanings appearing in VOLS. 1 and 3.

Parts One and Two follow, respectively, the methods of VOLS. 1 and 2 of *Remembering the Kanji*. The layout of the frames has changed slightly to include cross-referencing. Frames in Part One look like this:

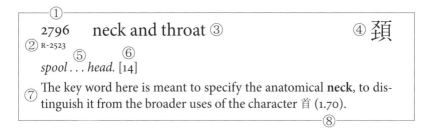

① Frame number. The enumeration is continued from VOL. 1.

② Frame number of reading. The corresponding frame appears in Part Two of the present volume, the enumeration continuing from VOL. 2.

③ Key word.

④ Kanji.

⑤ Primitive elements.

⑥ Number of strokes.

⑦ Explanatory note. *Italics* are used to refer to primitive element, **bold type** to the key word.

⑧ Cross-reference to VOL. and frame.

The frames of Part Two are patterned on the following sample:

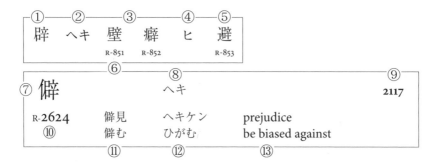

① Signal primitive for the following frames.

② Primary *on-yomi* of the signal primitive.

③ Kanji from VOL. 2 with the signal primitive and its primary *on-yomi*.

④ Secondary *on-yomi* of the signal primitive.

⑤ Kanji from VOL. 2 with the signal primitive and its secondary *on-yomi*.

⑥ Cross-reference to frame number in VOL. 2.

⑦ Kanji.

⑧ *On-yomi* of the frame kanji.

⑨ Cross-reference to frame in Part One.

⑩ Frame number for Part Two (reading). These numbers are continued from VOL. 1.

⑪ Sample compound and writing for *kun-yomi*.

⑫ Readings of sample compound and *kun-yomi*.

⑬ English translation of sample compound and Japanese meaning.

The choice of sample words for *on-yomi* readings has been made with an eye to providing useful vocabulary wherever possible, but here, too, there was some arbitrariness. In the course of assigning readings to the kanji, a shelf of dictionaries based on the JIS lists was consulted and compared, only to find inconsistencies at every turn. Given the ease with which computerized data can be accessed, one would expect at least an overall accuracy in indexing and cross-referencing. This was not the case. To compensate for this, Index 6 errs on the side of excess, including more readings than are mentioned in the frames of Part Two. The only exception was made for names: only those readings in the Ministry of Education's updated list are contained in the index.

Otherwise, all four indexes cover all the kanji and readings contained in the three volumes of the *Remembering the Kanji* series.

In conclusion, I should like to express my thanks to Torisawa Kazuko for her meticulous checking of the completed typescript, and to Pat Crosby of the University of Hawai'i Press for taking over the publication of this and other volumes in the series.

James W. Heisig
Nagoya

PART ONE

Writing

CHAPTER 1

New Primitives and Kanji Primitives

NEW PRIMITIVES

WE BEGIN our journey to 3,000 kanji with the addition of a few new primitive elements to those already included in VOL. 1. They have been included only if they appear frequently enough in the kanji in general to be useful, or if at least three instances appear in this volume. Each new element is followed by the new characters in which it appears.

After this, all the primitives in this volume will already be familiar to you. If you get stuck, consult the comprehensive list in Index II at the end of this volume.

2043 R-2670	this here	此
footprint . . . spoon. [6]		
2044 R-2671	brushwood	柴
this here . . . tree. [10]		
2045 R-2672	fort	砦
this here . . . stone. [11]		
2046 R-2673	whit	此二
this here . . . two. [8]		

| 2047 | beard | 髭 |

R-3140

hair . . . shape . . . this here. [16]

| ❖ | sheik | 离 |

top hat . . . villain . . . belt . . . elbow. [10]

This element is already familiar from the character 離 (1.1492). The reason the element for *elbow* requires 3 strokes instead of the usual 2 is that the combination of elements 内 is actually a radical classically defined as having 5 strokes.

| 2048 | crystal | 璃 |

R-2454

jewel . . . sheik. [15]

This is one of the seven classical stones of China.

| 2049 | fowl | 禽 |

R-2843

umbrella . . . sheik. [12]

| 2050 | apple | 檎 |

R-2844

tree . . . fowl. [16]

| ❖ | shoeshine | 舜 |

rice . . . sunglasses. [12]

This combination of elements has already been learned from the character 隣 (1.1311). The assignation of the primitive meaning is almost entirely arbitrary.

| 2051 | sympathize with | 憐 |

R-2499

state of mind . . . shoeshine. [15]

2052	phosphorus	燐
R-2496		

fire . . . shoeshine. [16]

2053	camelopard	麟
R-2498		

deer . . . shoeshine. [23]

The **camelopard** is a motley-colored mythical creature from China with the body of a *deer*, the tail of a cow, and the crest and claws of a bird.

2054	scaled	鱗
R-2497		

fish . . . shoeshine. [23]

The **scales** referred to are those found on fish, dragons, and so forth.

2055	encompassing	奄
R-2583		

St. Bernard . . . eel. [8]

The sense of the key word is of something that is expansive and covers over everything. When used as a primitive, it will mean a *dachshund*. Think here of a particularly large and l-o-n-g one to combine the qualities of the *eel* and the *St. Bernard*.

2056	hermitage	庵
R-2582		

cave . . . dachshund. [11]

2057	shrouded	掩
R-2584		

fingers . . . dachshund. [11]

The sense of the key word does not refer to an actually funeral "shroud," but only to the sense of being covered over or concealed.

2058	myself	俺
R-2585		

person . . . dachshund. [10]

The key word refers to a very familiar way of referring to oneself, usually restricted to men.

❖   streetwalker   夋

We learned this combination earlier in the character 俊 (1.1014) with the elements *person . . . license . . . walking legs.* The primitive meaning covers the sense of one "walking around licentiously." [7]

2059   **make amends**   悛
R-2501

state of mind . . . streetwalker. [10]

2060   **steed**   駿
R-2503

team of horses . . . streetwalker. [17]

2061   **steep**   峻
R-2500

mountain . . . streetwalker. [10]

2062   **complete a job**   竣
R-2502

vase . . . streetwalker. [12]

2063   **mortar**   臼
R-2973

back-to-back *staples.* [6]

The **mortar** referred to here is a stone or wooden basin used for grinding with a pestle. As a primitive element it keeps the same meaning.

2064   **father-in-law**   舅
R-3085

mortar . . . male. [13]

2065   **mouse**   鼠
R-2964

mortar . . . two plows . . . four drops . . . hook. [13]

2066 bore 鑿
R-3039

standing in a row upside down . . . mortar and walking stick . . . missile . . . metal. [28]

The sense of the key word is **boring** a hole into something.

2067 break 毀
R-3043

mortar . . . soil . . . missile. [13]

2068 small craft 艘
R-2383

boat . . . mortar . . . walking stick . . . crotch. [15]

❖ **I Ching** ䷿

The appearance of this element looks enough like one of the combinations used in the Chinese Book of Changes, the **I Ching**, to give us a meaning for this element. Note that there is always something that comes between the two halves to keep them apart. [4]

2069 rhinoceros 犀
R-3018

flag . . . I Ching . . . walking stick . . . cow. [12]

2070 lunar month 皐
R-3007

white dove . . . I Ching . . . needle. [11]

2071 spinal column 脊
R-2915

I Ching . . . umbrella . . . flesh. [10]

❖ **stitching** 叕

This element is actually a character in its own right, a pictograph of something that has been **stitched**. [8]

2072   rice-field footpath
R-3141

畷

field . . . stitching. [13]

The character learned for *paddy-ridge* in VOL. 1 畔 (1.1204) and that for *paddy-field ridge* 畦, which we will meet in FRAME 2571, both mean the "ridges" that run between rice paddies. The character introduced here refers directly to the ridge that is used as a walking path.

2073   mend
R-2918

綴

thread . . . stitching. [14]

2074   let it be
R-2473

爾

spike . . . eight . . . belt . . . stitching. [14]

Note that the writing of the element for *spike* is interrupted by the element for *eight*. This character—among whose older usages was as a polite form of addressing someone—is now used chiefly in names, except for the famous Buddhist expression that will be introduced when its reading comes up in Part Two.

2075   imperial seal
R-2474

璽

let it be . . . jewel. [19]

❖   hill of beans

豈

This element (actually a rather rare character in its own right) is made up of exactly what it says: a **hill of beans**. [10]

2076   suit of armor
R-2486

鎧

metal . . . hill of beans. [18]

2077   triumph
R-2485

凱

hill of beans . . . wind. [12]

❖   sapling 夭

drop . . . St. Bernard. [4]

This element is easily confused with the shape of the character 天 in such kanji as 添 (1.634) and in the element 喬 (1, page 158). Its meaning comes from the rather rare kanji on which it is based.

2078 bewitched 妖
R-2862

woman . . . sapling. [7]

2079 irrigate 沃
R-2861

water . . . sapling. [7]

2080 quaff 吞
R-2914

sapling . . . mouth. [7]

❖   green onion 韭

un- . . . floor. [9]

2081 leek 韮
R-3142

flowers . . . green onion. [12]

2082 lottery 籤
R-2835

bamboo . . . assembly line . . . fiesta . . . green onion. [23]

The character can also replace *assembly line* and *fiesta* with *Thanksgiving*: 簸. This alternate form is less common, however.

2083 penitential 懺
R-3047

state of mind . . . green onion. [20]

As in the previous frame, *assembly line* and *fiesta* can be replaced with *Thanksgiving*: 懴, though again less commonly.

2084 hay 窡
R-3047

Think of this element as showing two ricks of dried **hay** lying on top of each other. The element for *bound up* is familiar. The 3-stroked piece being bound up appeared in the primitive for *mountain goat* 芈. Think of the *goat* burying his "missing" horns in the **hay** to pick them up and toss them. [10]

2085 chick 雛
R-2466

hay . . . turkey. [18]

2086 scurry 趨
R-2465

run . . . hay. [17]

The sense of this key word is the way someone in kimono runs, taking short steps quickly.

2087 understandably 尤
R-3001

chihuahua with one human leg. [4]

The sense of the key word is that something "stands to reason."

2088 training 稽
R-3001

wheat . . . chihuahua with one human leg . . . delicious. [15]

2089 immense 厖
R-3035

cliff . . . chihuahua with one human leg . . . shape. [9]

NEW KANJI FROM OLD PRIMITIVES

We close this first chapter with a handful of kanji that are already familiar to you as primitive elements. The only thing you need to learn now is the meaning they take as kanji—not always the same as the meaning assigned them as primitives. Try to relate the two meanings together if this causes confusion.

2090 R-2565	**grab**	采

vulture . . . tree. [8]

We already met this combination in the characters 採, 菜, and 彩 (1.733, 734, 1714).

2091 R-3143	**a**	或

mouth . . . floor . . . fiesta. [8]

This character is roughly equivalent to the indefinite article *a* in English or to the phrase *a* certain.... It appears as a primitive in the characters 域 and 惑 (1.356, 614).

2092 R-2411	**chop off**	斬

car . . . axe. [11]

You may recall that this character already appeared as a combination of primitives in the character 暫 (1.1134).

2093 R-2839	**rabbit**	兎

drop of . . . day on its side . . . human legs . . . drop of. [8]

The older form from which the *rabbit* primitive was derived is actually 兔, but the abbreviation in this frame has, with the support of its listing in the first JIS list, come to take over. Note that the primitive for *rabbit* 免 (1, page 394) differs again from both of these by lacking the final stroke. To distinguish the first drop of from the last, you might think of the **rabbit's** long ears and short tail.

2094 *est* 也
R-2770

This is the element we learned as *scorpion*. We give the Latin word *est* as a key word to stress the "classical" flavor of the character, which appears today chiefly in names. [3]

2095 lofty 尭
R-2550

This was the primitive element we learned as *straw man*. [8]

2096 comma-design 巴
R-2762

The primitive meaning learned in VOL. 1, *mosaic*, is close to the meaning of the original character here, which is the shape of a "comma" used in heraldic designs, the most familiar of which has 3 "commas" swirling around each other. (If it is any help in remembering the character, one of the older meanings is an "elephant-eating snake.") [4]

2097 offspring 甫
R-2682

This character, none other than the element we learned as *dog tag*, is a nickname for a male child. It is used chiefly in personal names. [7]

2098 critters 疋
R-3144

Conveniently, the original kanji of the element we learned as *zoo* means a counter for animals in general. [5]

2099 violet 菫
R-2314

The element we learned as meaning *cabbage* comes from the kanji meaning for a **violet**. The addition of the fourth stroke appears in older forms of kanji that use this element also. Here you may think of it as a "purple *cabbage*" hanging on an overhead trestle of **violets** to recall the difference. [11]

| 2100 | mandala | 曼 |

R-2347

Since this character is most familiarly used in transcribing the Sanskrit word *mandala*, we shall allow its primitive meaning to stand as the key word for the kanji also. [11]

| 2101 | towel | 巾 |

R-3019

If we allow the full range of original meanings for the English word **towel**, which includes cleaning cloths, covering cloths, and strips of cloth used in clothing, we can keep the primitive meaning for the key word here. [3]

| 2102 | quote | 云 |

R-2848

The primitive we learned as *rising cloud* is actually a kanji used to indicate someone's spoken words. [4]

| 2103 | augury | |

R-2442

The primitive meaning of *magic wand* is not far from the sense of the original kanji here. [2]

| 2104 | heaven-high | 喬 |

R-2350

This character was learned as the primitive *angel*. [12]

| 2105 | shalt | |

R-2551

The key word here is meant to suggest the "Thou **shalt**" and "Thou **shalt** not" of the commandments. [10]

CHAPTER 2

Major Primitive Elements

THE KANJI treated in this chapter comprise the bulk of PART ONE of this book, some 734 characters in all. Each character is entered under its principal primitive element, and the elements themselves are arranged in their dictionary order.

亻 PERSON

2106 R-2534	**Yamato**	倭
person . . . committee. [10]		
2107 R-2265	**chivalry**	侠
person . . . scissors. [8]		
2108 R-2549	**fed up**	倦
person . . . scroll. [11]		
2109 R-2504	**comely**	佼
person . . . mingle. [8]		
2110 R-2286	**abrupt**	俄
person . . . ego. [9]		
2111 R-2789	**work a field**	佃
person . . . field. [7]		

2112 R-2491	minstrel	伶
person . . . orders. [7]		

2113 R-2795	animal offspring	仔
person . . . child. [5]		

2114 R-2788	foe	仇
person . . . baseball team. [4]		

2115 R-2685	look after	伽
person . . . add. [7]		

2116 R-2313	trifle	僅
person . . . cabbage. [12]		

2117 R-2624	biased	僻
person . . . ketchup. [15]		

2118 R-2738	make a profit	儲
person . . . various. [17]		
If it helps, you can also read the primitives as *believe . . . puppet.*		

2119 R-2461	bliss	倖
person . . . happiness. [10]		

2120 R-2349	emigrant	僑
person . . . angel. [14]		

2121 R-2790	partner	侶
person . . . spine. [9]		

2122 R-2754	performing artist	伎
person . . . branch. [6]		

2123 R-2969	integrity	侃
person . . . mouth . . . flood. [8]		

2124 R-3022	mate	倶
person . . . tool. [10]		

2125 R-3145	as is	儘
person . . . exhaust. [8]		

2126 R-2648	adjutant	佑
person . . . right. [7]		

2127 R-3146	fork in a road	俣
person . . . mouth . . . heaven. [9]		

2128 R-2406	hire	傭
person . . . commonplace. [13]		

2129 R-2423	memorial	偲
person . . . think. [11]		

2130	**dried meat**	脩
R-2852		

person ... walking stick ... taskmaster ... meat. [11]

2131	**my son**	倅
R-3051		

person ... graduate. [10]

2132	**make do**	做
R-3137		

person ... happenstance. [11]

The key word combines the meanings of the character for **make** 作 (1.1142) and 為 **do** (1.1918).

冫 ICE

2133	**nifty**	凄
R-2390		

ice ... wife. [10]

2134	**sharp**	冴
R-2667		

ice ... tusk. [7]

The sense of this key word is broad enough to include "bright," "clear," and "on one's toes."

2135	**wilt**	凋
R-2766		

ice ... circumference. [10]

2136	**pull through**	凌
R-2353		

ice ... rice-seedling ... walking legs. [10]

2137 R-2654	metallurgy	冶
	ice . . . pedestal. [7]	
2138 R-3045	stately	凛
	ice . . . -times . . . altar. [15]	

几 WIND

2139 R-3105	kite	凧
	wind . . . towel. [5]	
2140 R-3104	lull	凪
	wind . . . stop. [6]	
2141 R-2946	earlybird	夙
	wind . . . bone. [6]	
2142 R-2934	phoenix	鳳
	wind . . . ceiling . . . bird. [14]	

刂 SABRE

2143 R-2528	slaughter	劉
	receipt . . . sword . . . metal . . . sabre. [15]	

2144	moment	刹

R-3042

sheaf . . . tree . . . sabre. [8]

The key word here is the noun meaning "a brief **moment**."

2145	peel off	剥

R-2912

broom . . . rice grains . . . saber. [10]

2146	shave	剃

R-2639

younger brother . . . saber. [9]

勹 BOUND UP

2147	aroma	匂

R-3103

bound up . . . spoon. [4]

2148	flexed	勾

R-2842

bound up . . . elbow. [4]

厂 CLIFF

2149	despondent	厭

R-2933

cliff . . . wagging tongue . . . moon . . . dog. [14]

This character, which carries the sense of being weighted down by the meaninglessness of life, calls to mind a vivid image of despair in Nietzsche's *Thus Spoke Zarathustra* that makes it simple to remember. Walking the dark *cliffs* at midnight, Zarathustra hears a *dog* howling. He approaches, and under the light of the *moon* sees a shepherd lad lying on the ground with a thick, black snake hanging out of his mouth (like a long, *wagging tongue*, we might add). The snake had crawled in while he was asleep and grabbed on to the lad's throat. Zarathustra tells him to bite off the head of the snake and become free of the despair that holds him in tortured captivity.

2150 R-2596	**wild goose**	雁
cliff ... person ... turkey. [12]		
2151 R-2595	**counterfeit**	贋
wild goose ... money. [19]		
2152 R-2866	**kitchen**	厨
cliff ... table ... glue. [12]		
2153 R-3055	**insinuate**	仄
cliff ... person. [4]		

口 MOUTH

2154 R-2627	**scout**	哨
mouth ... candle. [10]		
2155 R-2578	**derision**	嘲
mouth ... morning. [15]		

2156 R-3036	reprehend	咎
walking legs . . . person . . . mouth. [8]		

2157 R-3135	whisper	囁
mouth . . . three ears. [21]		

2158 R-2506	chatter	喋
mouth . . . generations . . . tree. [12]		

2159 R-2598	windpipe	咽
mouth . . . cause. [9]		

2160 R-2373	quarrel	嘩
mouth . . . splendid. [13]		

2161 R-3147	gossip	噂
mouth . . . revered. [15]		

2162 R-2768	cough	咳
mouth . . . acorn. [9]		

2163 R-3024	clamor	喧
mouth . . . proclaim. [12]		

2164 R-2328	throat	喉
mouth . . . marquis. [12]		

2165	saliva	唾
R-2679		
	mouth . . . droop. [11]	

2166	bash	叩
R-2923		
	mouth . . . stamp. [5]	

2167	fib	嘘
R-2571		
	mouth . . . void. [14]	

2168	peck at	啄
R-2929		
	mouth . . . sow. [10]	

2169	curse	呪
R-2930		
	mouth . . . older brother. [8]	

2170	barking	吠
R-2931		
	mouth . . . chihuahua. [7]	

2171	dangle	吊
R-3056		
	mouth . . . towel. [6]	

2172	chew	噛
R-3148		
	mouth . . . teeth. [15]	

2173	within my ability	叶
R-3057		
	mouth . . . needle. [5]	

| 2174
R-2967 | sides of the mouth | 吻 |

mouth ... knot. [7]

| 2175
R-2876 | stammer | 吃 |

mouth ... beg. [6]

| 2176
R-3149 | spin a tale | 嘶 |

mouth ... new. [16]

| 2177
R-2646 | miso | 噌 |

mouth ... increase. [14]

Miso is the fermented soybean paste commonly used in Japanese cooking as a base for soups and stews.

| 2178
R-2459 | pop song | 唄 |

mouth ... shell. [10]

This character was originally used to indicate songs accompanied by the shamisen but now most commonly refers to **pop songs**.

| 2179
R-2924 | scold | 叱 |

mouth ... diced. [5]

| 2180
R-3058 | city walls | 邑 |

mouth ... mosaic. [7]

This is the parent character from which the primitive 巴 is derived.

| 2181
R-3052 | dumbfounded | 呆 |

mouth ... tree. [7]

2182	ingest	喰
R-3150		
mouth ... eat. [12]		

土 SOIL

2183	clay	埴
R-2708		
soil ... straightaway. [11]		

2184	authochthonous	坤
R-2569		
soil ... monkey. [8]		
In Chinese astrology and divining, this character refers to "the earthly" and stands counter to 乾 as the "moist" against the "dry."		

2185	piled high	堆
R-2783		
soil ... turkey. [11]		

2186	dugout	壕
R-2379		
soil ... overpowering. [17]		
Compare 濠 (FRAME 2306).		

2187	blemish	垢
R-2409		
soil ... empress. [9]		

2188	flat	坦
R-2554		
soil ... nightbreak. [8]		

2189 R-2482	wharf	埠
soil . . . large city. [11]		

2190 R-2694	stuff up	填
soil . . . true. [13]		

2191 R-2432	dam	堰
soil . . . box . . . sun . . . woman. [12]		

2192 R-2739	railing	堵
soil . . . puppet. [12]		

女 WOMAN

2193 R-2968	suckling infant	嬰
two shells . . . woman. [17]		

2194 R-2928	violate	姦
three women. [9]		

2195 R-2902	jealous	妬
woman . . . rock. [8]		

2196 R-2621	handmaiden	婢
woman . . . lowly. [11]		

2197 well finished
R-2635

woman . . . address. [11]

婉

2198 harlot
R-2268

woman . . . prosperous. [11]

娼

2199 courtesan
R-2755

woman . . . branch. [7]
Take care not to confuse with **harlot** in the previous frame.

妓

2200 fair
R-2753

woman . . . ivy. [9]
The sense here is of someone lovely to behold.

娃

2201 niece
R-3020

woman . . . climax. [9]

姪

2202 envy
R-2429

woman . . . rapidly. [13]

嫉

2203 mistress
R-2305

woman . . . demand. [17]
The sense of the key word here is the feminine form of "master."

嬬

2204 aged woman
R-3089

woman . . . old man. [9]

姥

2205 R-2657	**mother-in-law** *woman . . . old.* [8]	姑
2206 R-3119	**young miss** *woman . . . shelf.* [8]	姐
2207 R-2403	**overjoyed** *woman . . . rejoice.* [15]	嬉

子 CHILD

2208 R-3136	**expecting** *fist . . . child.* [5] The key word here means "pregnant."	孕
2209 R-2885	**assiduous** *child . . . taskmaster.* [7]	孜

宀 HOUSE

2210 R-2841	**soothe** *house . . . possession.* [9]	宥

2211 R-2724	**imply**	寓
	house . . . Talking Cricket. [12]	
2212 R-2613	**extensive**	宏
	house . . . by one's side . . . elbow. [7]	
2213 R-2927	**jail**	牢
	house . . . cow. [7]	
2214 R-2926	**block up**	塞
	house . . . celery . . . animal legs . . . soil. [13]	
2215 R-2925	**Sung dynasty**	宋
	house . . . tree. [7]	
2216 R-3111	**venison**	宍
	house . . . six. [7]	
	This character is used for the meat of wild animals in general, particularly boar and deer—hence the choice of the key word.	

尸 FLAG

2217 R-2740	**butchering**	屠
	flag . . . puppet. [11]	
2218 R-2630	**fart**	屁
	flag . . . compare. [7]	

2219 rubbish R-2628 *flag . . . candle.* [10]	屑
2220 buttocks R-3151 *flag . . . baseball team.* [5]	尻
2221 frequently R-2988 *flag . . . rice . . . woman.* [12]	屢
2222 corpse R-2792 *flag . . . death.* [9]	屍
2223 folding screen R-2513 *flag . . . puzzle.* [9]	屏

山 MOUNTAIN

2224 high-reaching R-2513 *mountain . . . tall.* [13]	嵩
2225 rugged mountains R-2354 *mountain . . . rice-seedlings . . . walking legs.* [11]	崚
2226 high mountain R-2287 *mountain . . . ego.* [10]	峨

2227	bluffs	崖
R-2441		

mountain . . . cliff . . . ivy. [11]

2228	mountaintop	嶺
R-2495		

mountain . . . jurisdiction. [17]

2229	fit into	嵌
R-2555		

mountain . . . wicker basket . . . yawn. [12]
This character is used to express **fitting** one thing **into** another.

2230	rocky	嵯
R-2364		

mountain . . . discrimination. [13]

巾 TOWEL

2231	quire	帖
R-2878		

towel . . . fortuneteller. [8]
The key word here is a counter for 25 sheets of paper.

2232	banner	幡
R-3152		

towel . . . dice. [15]

2233	pennant	幟
R-2756		

towel . . . kazoo. [15]

广 CAVE

2234 R-2249	cleaver	庖
	cave . . . wrap. [8]	
2235 R-2451	licensed quarters	廓
	cave . . . enclosure. [14]	
2236 R-2629	overhang	庇
	cave . . . compare. [7]	
2237 R-2597	hawk	鷹
	cave . . . person . . . turkey . . . bird. [24]	
2238 R-3059	shire	庄
	cave . . . soil. [6]	
2239 R-2577	tomb sanctuary	廟
	cave . . . morning. [15]	

弓 BOW

2240 R-2830	strengthen	彊
	bow . . . 2 fields . . . floors and ceilings. [16] See FRAME 2509 for a similar right-side combination.	

2241 R-2892	more and more	弥
	bow . . . reclining . . . small. [8]	
2242 R-2771	loosen	弛
	bow . . . scorpion. [6]	
2243 R-3113	rice gruel	粥
	rice between two bows. [12]	

扌 FINGERS

2244 R-2723	lathe	挽
	fingers . . . rabbit. [11]	
2245 R-2318	bump into	撞
	fingers . . . juvenile. [15]	
2246 R-2678	disguise	扮
	fingers . . . part. [7]	
2247 R-2744	pillage	掠
	fingers . . . capital. [11]	
2248 R-3060	shove	挨
	fingers . . . elbow . . . dart. [10]	

2249 R-3025	clutch	掴
fingers . . . country. [11]		
2250 R-2910	impress	捺
fingers . . . Nara. [11] The **impression** referred to here is like that made by a seal on wax.		
2251 R-2574	wrenching	捻
fingers . . . wish. [11]		
2252 R-2380	scratch	掻
fingers . . . crotch . . . insect. [11]		
2253 R-2358	assortment	撰
fingers . . . two snakes . . . strung together. [15]		
2254 R-2987	wipe	拭
fingers . . . style. [9]		
2255 R-2619	muster	揃
fingers . . . in front. [12] The sense of the key word here is "assembling in an orderly fashion."		
2256 R-3153	deal with	捌
fingers . . . separate. [10]		
2257 R-2417	churn up	撹
fingers . . . memorize. [15]		

2258 R-3154	rubbing	摺

fingers . . . learn. [14]
The sense here is of **rubbing** out an image, as in "brass-**rubbing**."

2259 R-2289	press down on	按

fingers . . . relax. [9]

2260 R-2330	nab	捉

fingers . . . wooden leg. [10]

2261 R-3015	imminent	拶

fingers . . . flood . . . evening. [9]

2262 R-2731	disseminate	播

fingers . . . dice. [15]

2263 R-2591	collect	揖

fingers . . . mouth . . . ear. [12]
The sense of the key word is to compile or bring together.

2264 R-2337	receptacle	托

fingers . . . lock of hair. [6]

2265 R-2518	devote	捧

fingers . . . dedicate. [11]

2266 R-2323	twirl	撚

fingers . . . sort of a thing. [15]

2267   counter for tools   挺
R-2276

fingers . . . courts. [10]
This character is for counting scissors, guns, inksticks, oars, etc.

2268   commotion   擾
R-2568

fingers . . . melancholy. [18]

2269   make headway   捗
R-2996

fingers . . . walk. [11]

2270   petting   撫
R-2608

fingers . . . non. [15]

2271   sprinkle   撒
R-2970

fingers . . . scatter. [15]

2272   outstanding   擢
R-2995

fingers . . . feathers . . . turkey. [17]
The concept here is "conspicuously surpass," or "stick out of the crowd."

2273   spoils   捷
R-2879

fingers . . . broom run. [11]
Take special care when writing the right side of this character. The first stroke belongs to the element *run* and is followed by that for *broom*.

2274   gouge out   抉
R-2532

fingers . . . guillotine. [7]

忄 STATE OF MIND

2275 R-2864	wince	怯
state of mind . . . gone. [8]		
2276 R-2787	ponder	惟
state of mind . . . turkey. [11]		
2277 R-2487	infatuation	惚
state of mind . . . knot . . . heart. [11]		
2278 R-2492	quickwitted	怜
state of mind . . . orders. [8]		
2279 R-2676	considerate	怜
state of mind . . . receive. [11]		
2280 R-2317	yearn	憧
state of mind . . . juvenile. [15]		
2281 R-2665	as if	恰
state of mind . . . fit. [9]		
2282 R-2832	enlarge	恢
state of mind . . . ashes. [9]		

| 2283 | respect for elders | 悌 |
| R-2640 | | |

state of mind . . . younger brother. [10]

氵 WATER

| 2284 | bubble up | 湧 |
| R-2405 | | |

water . . . courageous. [12]

| 2285 | canal | 澪 |
| R-2493 | | |

water . . . rain . . . orders. [16]

| 2286 | glistening | 洸 |
| R-2793 | | |

water . . . ray. [9]

| 2287 | bounding main | 滉 |
| R-2478 | | |

water . . . sun . . . ray. [13]
The sense of the key word is of a vast and deep body of *water*.

| 2288 | gargle | 漱 |
| R-3049 | | |

water . . . bundle . . . yawn. [14]

| 2289 | continent | 洲 |
| R-2322 | | |

water . . . state. [9]

| 2290 | swirling waters | 洵 |
| R-2580 | | |

water . . . decameron. [9]

2291	**seep**	滲
R-2775		
water . . . nonplussed. [14]		
2292	**rinse**	洒
R-2801		
water . . . west. [9]		
2293	**douse**	沐
R-2799		
water . . . tree. [7]		
2294	**teardrops**	泪
R-2820		
water . . . eye. [8]		
2295	**gushing**	渾
R-2759		
water . . . chariot. [12]		
2296	**grains of sand**	沙
R-2452		
water . . . few. [7]		
2297	**blaspheme**	涜
R-2802		
water . . . sell. [10]		
2298	**lewd**	淫
R-2850		
water . . . vulture . . . porter. [11]		
2299	**roofbeam**	梁
R-2900		
water . . . sword . . . two drops . . . tree. [11]		

| 2300 | sediment | | 澱 |
| R-2407 | | | |

water ... Mr. [16]

| 2301 | widespread | | 氾 |
| R-2443 | | | |

water ... fingerprint. [5]

| 2302 | old Kyoto | | 洛 |
| R-2741 | | | |

water ... each. [9]

This kanji originally referred to a place name in China, but in Japan was adopted to refer to Kyoto, where it still survives in the names of places and traditional establishments.

| 2303 | thou | | 汝 |
| R-2798 | | | |

water ... woman. [6]

| 2304 | filter | | 漉 |
| R-2370 | | | |

water ... deer. [14]

| 2305 | on the verge of | | 瀬 |
| R-2435 | | | |

water ... repeatedly. [19]

| 2306 | moat | | 濠 |
| R-2378 | | | |

water ... overpowering. [17]

This character, used today as an abbreviation for the country of Australia, should be learned in connection with 壕 (FRAME 2186).

| 2307 | spray | | 洗 |
| R-2535 | | | |

water ... discharge. [12]

2308 R-2940	**drowning**	溺
water . . . weak. [13] Do not confuse with 没 (1.707), which is closer to the sense of founder.		
2309 R-2439	**port**	湊
water . . . play music. [12]		
2310 R-2445	**solitude**	淋
water . . . grove. [11]		
2311 R-2941	**abounding**	浩
water . . . revelation. [10]		
2312 R-2706	**water's edge**	汀
water . . . spike. [5]		
2313 R-2808	**large goose**	鴻
water . . . craft . . . bird. [17]		
2314 R-2536	**souse**	潅
water . . . pegasus. [14]		
2315 R-2953	**brimming**	溢
water . . . benefit. [13]		
2316 R-2433	**cleanse**	汰
water . . . plump. [7]		

| 2317 R-3017 | inundate | 湛 |
| water . . . tremendously. [12] | | |

| 2318 R-2674 | immaculate | 淳 |
| water . . . receive. [11] | | |

| 2319 R-2826 | defile | 瀆 |
| water . . . precious. [15] | | |

| 2320 R-2547 | moisten | 渥 |
| water . . . roof. [12] | | |

| 2321 R-2805 | rough seas | 灘 |
| water . . . difficult. [21] | | |

| 2322 R-2271 | draw water | 汲 |
| water . . . reach out. [6] | | |

| 2323 R-3126 | river pool | 潚 |
| water . . . silent. [17] | | |

| 2324 R-2529 | cumulation | 溜 |
| water . . . detain. [13] | | |

| 2325 R-2952 | abyss | 渕 |
| water . . . golden calf . . . sabre. [11] | | |

2326 R-2610	chaos	沌
	water . . . earthworm. [7]	

2327 R-2545	pan-	汎

water . . . mediocre. [6]

The sense of the key word here is the "all" as in terms like **Pan**-American. It is also the character used in mathematics for "partial" as in partial differentials.

2328 R-2863	strainer	濾
	water . . . prudence. [18]	

2329 R-2306	drench	濡
	water . . . demand. [17]	

2330 R-3155	eddy	淀
	water . . . determine. [11]	

2331 R-3061	fabrication	涅

water . . . sun . . . soil. [9]

The key word here is meant to suggest not merely something made, but something made with an intention to deceive.

父 FATHER

2332 R-2813	cauldron	釜

father . . . metal. [10]

Note the stroke overlap between *father* and *metal*.

2333 R-2814	hatchet	斧
father ... axe. [8]		
2334 R-2468	grandpa	爺
father ... ear ... city walls. [13]		

犭 PACK OF WILD DOGS

2335 R-2522	sly	猾
pack of wild dogs ... skeleton. [13]		
2336 R-2587	indecent	猥
pack of wild dogs ... be apprehensive. [12]		
2337 R-2505	cunning	狡
pack of wild dogs ... mingle. [9]		
2338 R-2600	racoon dog	狸
pack of wild dogs ... computer. [10]		
2339 R-2603	wolf	狼
pack of wild dogs ... halo. [10]		
2340 R-2460	flustered	狽
pack of wild dogs ... shellfish. [10]		

2341 R-2444	pup	狗
pack of wild dogs . . . phrase. [8]		

2342 R-2510	fox	狐
pack of wild dogs . . . melon. [8]		

2343 R-2244	*a-un*	狛
pack of wild dogs . . . white. [8]		

The **a-un** are lion-like dogs that often grace the front of temples or public buildings in Japan. Their name comes from the first and last letters of the Sanskrit alphabet (transliterated in Japanese as 阿吽) and symbolize a wholeness as in the English phrase "alpha and omega."

2344 R-2253	aim at	狙
pack of wild dogs . . . shelf. [8]		

2345 R-2424	lion	獅
pack of wild dogs . . . expert. [13]		

2346 R-2546	baboon	狒
pack of wild dogs . . . dollar sign. [8]		

艹 FLOWERS

2347 R-3156	tobacco	莨
flowers . . . good. [8]		

2348   jasmine
R-2279

flowers . . . extremity. [8]

茉

2349   hawthorn
R-2280

flowers . . . profit. [10]

莉

2350   strawberry
R-3138

flowers . . . mother. [8]

苺

Note that the element for mother is written in its full form, not the normal abbreviated form it usually takes when used as a primitive. To help remember this, think of the original pictographic image of the "two breasts of the *mother.*"

2351   bush clover
R-2308

flowers . . . autumn. [12]

萩

2352   technique [old]
R-3183

flowers . . . rice-seedlings . . . ground . . . fat man . . . rising cloud. [18]
The abbreviation in common use is 芸 (1.421).

藝

2353   trim
R-3157

flowers . . . pheasant. [16]
The second element appears in FRAME 2584.

薙

2354   straw raincoat
R-3158

flowers . . . declining. [13]

蓑

2355   numb
R-2533

flowers . . . committee. [11]

萎

| 2356 | moss | 苔 |
| R-2656 | | |

flowers . . . pedestal. [8]

| 2357 | prodigal | 蕩 |
| R-2450 | | |

flowers . . . hot water. [15]

| 2358 | cover over | 蔽 |
| R-2320 | | |

flower . . . shredder. [15]

| 2359 | tendril | 蔓 |
| R-2348 | | |

flowers . . . mandala. [14]

| 2360 | lotus | 蓮 |
| R-2463 | | |

flowers . . . carry along. [13]

| 2361 | lotus flower | 芙 |
| R-2517 | | |

flowers . . . husband. [7]

Even though there is no essential difference in meaning between this kanji and those in the preceding and following frames, the character 蓮 is the most common of the three.

| 2362 | lotus blossom | 蓉 |
| R-2300 | | |

flowers . . . contain. [13]

| 2363 | orchid | 蘭 |
| R-2400 | | |

flowers . . . gates . . . east. [19]

2364 R-2871	hollow reed	芦
flowers . . . door. [7]		

2365 R-2735	yam	薯
flowers . . . signature. [16]		

2366 R-2267	iris	菖
flowers . . . prosperous. [11]		

2367 R-2310	banana	蕉
flowers . . . char. [15]		

2368 R-2806	wick	芯
flowers . . . heart. [7]		

2369 R-2351	buckwheat	蕎
flowers . . . angel. [15]		

2370 R-2298	butterbur	蕗
flowers . . . path. [16]		

2371 R-2638	indigo	藍
flowers . . . oversee. [18]		

2372 R-2687	eggplant	茄
flowers . . . add. [8]		

2373 R-2250	bullying	苛
flowers ... can. [8]		

2374 R-2404	behind the scenes	蔭
flowers ... shade. [14]		

2375 R-2283	wormwood	蓬
flower ... tryst. [13]		

2376 R-2334	mustard	芥
flowers ... jammed in. [7]		

2377 R-2954	germinate	萌
flowers ... bright. [11]		

2378 R-2680	grape	葡
flowers ... bound up ... dog tag. [12]		

2379 R-2955	grape vine	萄
flowers ... bound up ... tin can. [11]		

2380 R-2962	resurrect	蘇
flowers ... fish ... wheat. [19]		

2381 R-2730	grow wild	蕃
flowers ... dice. [15]		

| 2382 | cocklebur | 苓 |

R-2490

flowers . . . orders. [8]

| 2383 | rush mat | 菰 |

R-2509

flowers . . . orphan. [11]

| 2384 | darken | 蒙 |

R-3011

flowers . . . crown . . . ceiling . . . sow. [13]

| 2385 | grassy reed | 茅 |

R-2994

flowers . . . halberd. [8]

| 2386 | plantain | 芭 |

R-2764

flowers . . . mosaic. [7]

| 2387 | mow | 苅 |

R-3131

flowers . . . reap. [7]

| 2388 | lid | 蓋 |

R-2984

flowers . . . gone . . . dish. [13]

| 2389 | onion | 葱 |

R-3062

flowers . . . double knot . . . heart. [12]

The double knot is from the extra stroke in the second primitive.

| 2390 | revile | 蔑 |

R-2982

flowers . . . net . . . a march. [14]

2391 R-3063	**hollyhock**	葵
	flowers ... teepee ... heaven. [12]	
2392 R-2589	**shingling**	葺
	flowers ... mouth ... ear. [12]	
2393 R-2822	**stamen**	蕊
	flowers ... three hearts. [15]	
2394 R-2873	**mushroom**	茸
	flowers ... ear. [9]	
2395 R-2716	**sowing**	蒔
	flowers ... time. [13]	
2396 R-2855	**parsley**	芹
	flowers ... axe. [7]	
2397 R-3125	**thatching**	苫
	flowers ... fortune-telling. [8]	
2398 R-2662	**kudzu**	葛
	flowers ... siesta. [11]	
2399 R-2296	**pale blue**	蒼
	flowers ... godown. [13]	

2400 straw R-3122 *flowers ... tall ... tree.* [17]		藁
2401 turnip R-2609 *flowers ... nothingness.* [15]		蕪
2402 sweet potato R-2736 *flowers ... words ... puppet.* [18]		藷
2403 quack R-2966 *flowers ... number.* [16] The key word here refers to a medic of questionable reputation. It does not, however, carry the original meaning of the German term: a doctor who used water to cure.		薮
2404 garlic R-3117 *flowers ... two altars.* [13]		蒜
2405 bracken R-3159 *flowers ... cliff ... mountain goat ... yawn.* [15]		蕨
2406 grow plentiful R-2559 *flower ... lieutenant.* [14]		蔚
2407 madder red R-2992 *flowers ... west.* [9]		茜

2408 R-2398	candle rush	莞
flowers . . . perfect. [10]		
2409 R-2829	collector	蒐
flowers . . . ghost. [13]		
2410 R-2256	sedge	菅
flowers . . . bureaucrat. [11]		
2411 R-2661	ditch reed	葦
flowers . . . locket. [12]		

辶 ROAD

2412 R-2778	Way	迪
road . . . sprout. [8] The upper case indicates its meaning as a true or moral **Way**.		
2413 R-3114	track down	辿
mountain . . . road. [6]		
2414 R-3064	crawl	這
words . . . road. [10]		
2415 R-2393	detour	迂
potato . . . road. [6]		

2416 shirk R-2561	遁
road . . . shield. [12]	
2417 tryst R-2282	逢
walking legs . . . bushes . . . road. [10]	
2418 far off R-2315	遥
condor . . . road. [12]	
2419 faraway R-2263	遼
road . . . pup tent. [15]	
2420 pressing R-2704	逼
wealth . . . road. [12]	
2421 until R-3160	迄
beg . . . road. [6]	
2422 modest R-2399	遜
grandchild . . . road. [13]	
2423 standstill R-2727	逗
table . . . road. [10]	

阝 CITY WALLS

2424 cultured R-3008	郁
possess . . . town walls. [9]	
2425 courtesy R-2908	鄭
animal horns . . . whiskey bottle . . . St. Bernard . . . city walls. [15]	

阝 PINNACLE

2426 chink R-2978	隙
pinnacle . . . small . . . sun . . . small. [12]	
2427 nook R-2586	隈
pinnacle . . . field . . . hairpin. [11]	

心 HEART

2428 possessed R-3041	憑
ice . . . team of horses . . . heart. [16] The key word here means "bewitched" or "enchanted" by a spirit.	
2429 attract R-2747	惹
young . . . heart. [12]	

| 2430
R-2566 | without exception | 悉 |

animal footprints . . . heart. [11]

| 2431
R-2488 | instantaneously | 忽 |

knot . . . heart. [8]

| 2432
R-2824 | firstborn son | 惣 |

thing . . . heart. [12]

| 2433
R-2261 | in the nick of time | 愈 |

butchers . . . heart. [13]

| 2434
R-2427 | sensitive | 恕 |

likeness . . . heart. [10]

日 SUN

| 2435
R-3046 | overarching | 昴 |

sun . . . receipt . . . stamp. [9]

Although this character is not essentially different in connotation from 昂 (FRAME 2449), it is used chiefly now in names.

| 2436
R-2833 | progress | 晋 |

The element for *sun* at the bottom is easy enough. The problem is that the top element, *row*, is an exception to the rule (1.1785) that the two *horns* at the top are eliminated only when it appears beneath its relative primitive. [10]

| 2437 | equivocal | 曖 |

R-2436

sun . . . love. [17]

| 2438 | aglow | 晟 |

R-2647

sun . . . turn into. [11]

| 2439 | halo | 暈 |

R-2758

sun atop a *chariot.* [13]

Be careful to keep this character distinct from that in the following frame, which differs only by the disposition of the elements.

| 2440 | glitter | 暉 |

R-2760

sun alongside a *chariot.* [13]

| 2441 | dry weather | 旱 |

R-2651

sun . . . clothesline. [7]

| 2442 | clear skies | 晏 |

R-2291

sun . . . relax. [10]

| 2443 | morrow | 晨 |

R-2512

sun . . . sign of the dragon. [11]

To indicate that this character is now used mainly in names, we have assigned it the somewhat archaic-sounding key word **morrow**.

| 2444 | bleaching | 晒 |

R-3128

sun . . . west. [10]

2445 obscure R-2537	昧

sun . . . not yet. [9]

2446 limpid R-2477	晃

sun . . . ray. [10]

2447 air out R-2338	曝

sun . . . outburst. [19]

2448 dawn R-2734	曙

sun . . . signature. [17]

2449 elevate R-2935	昂

sun . . . craft . . . seal. [8]

Although this character is not essentially different in connotation from 昂 (FRAME 2435), be sure to keep the writing distinct.

2450 effulgent R-2804	旺

sun . . . king. [8]

2451 dusk R-2457	昏

family name . . . sun. [8]

2452 last day of the month R-2773	晦

sun . . . every. [10]

月 FLESH·MOON

2453 R-2975	**kidney** *slave . . . crotch . . . flesh.* [13]	腎
2454 R-2895	**thigh** *flesh . . . missile.* [8]	股
2455 R-2331	**pus** *flesh . . . agriculture.* [17]	膿
2456 R-2255	**viscera** *flesh . . . borough.* [12]	腑
2457 R-2794	**bladder** *flesh . . . ray.* [10]	胱
2458 R-2870	**embryo** *flesh . . . negative.* [9]	胚
2459 R-2344	**anus** *flesh . . . craft.* [7]	肛
2460 R-2516	**cowardice** *flesh . . . idea.* [17]	臆

2461	knee	膝

R-2430

flesh . . . tree . . . umbrella . . . rice grains. [15]
Compare the right side of this character with 漆 (1.932).

2462	fragile	脆

R-2553

flesh . . . dangerous. [10]

2463	rib	肋

R-2981

flesh . . . power. [6]

2464	elbow	肘

R-2980

flesh . . . glue. [7]

2465	body cavity	腔

R-2888

flesh . . . empty. [12]

2466	gland	腺

R-2336

flesh . . . spring. [13]

2467	tumor	腫

R-2884

flesh . . . heavy. [13]

2468	dining tray	膳

R-2335

flesh . . . virtuous. [16]

2469	armrest	肱

R-2615

flesh . . . by one's side . . . elbow. [8]

| 2470 | uncivilized | 胡 |

R-2605

old . . . moon. [9]

This character referred in China to foreigners, especially those to the north and south of the "civilized" peoples who controlled the meaning of the characters. See FRAME 2881 for the Japanese equivalent.

木 TREE

| 2471 | maple tree | 楓 |

R-2526

tree . . . wind. [13]

| 2472 | pillow | 枕 |

R-3021

tree . . . crown tied around leg of person. [8]
Compare 沈 (1.1688).

| 2473 | purple willow | 楊 |

R-2733

tree . . . piggy bank. [13]

| 2474 | Oriental elm | 椋 |

R-2745

tree . . . capitol. [12]

| 2475 | hazel | 榛 |

R-2484

tree . . . bonsai . . . wheat. [14]

| 2476 | comb | 櫛 |

R-2942

tree . . . node. [17]

2477 R-2386	**wooden hammer**	槌
tree . . . chase. [13]		
2478 R-2309	**mallet**	樵
tree . . . char. [16]		
2479 R-2641	**ladder**	梯
tree . . . younger brother. [11]		
2480 R-2542	**chair**	椅
tree . . . strange. [12]		
2481 R-2538	**persimmon**	柿
tree . . . market. [9]		
2482 R-2556	**citrus tree**	柑
tree . . . sweet. [9]		
2483 R-3161	**girder**	桁
tree . . . going. [10]		
2484 R-2273	**picket**	杭
tree . . . whirlwind. [8]		
2485 R-2875	**holly**	柊
tree . . . winter. [9]		

2486	citron	柚
R-2779		
tree . . . sprout. [9]		

2487	wooden bowl	椀
R-2633		
tree . . . address. [12]		

2488	hemlock	栂
R-3109		
tree . . . mother. [9]		

2489	spindle tree	柾
R-3107		
tree . . . correct. [9]		

2490	sacred Shinto tree	榊
R-3106		
tree . . . gods. [13]		

2491	evergreen oak	樫
R-3098		
tree . . . strict. [16]		

2492	Chinese black pine	槙
R-2692		
tree . . . true. [14]		

2493	Japanese oak	楢
R-2818		
tree . . . animal horns . . . whisky bottle. [13]		

2494	mandarin orange	橘
R-2960		
tree . . . halbard . . . hood . . . human legs . . . mouth. [16]		

2495	Japanese cypress	桧

R-2333

tree ... meeting. [10]

See also FRAME 2964 for old form.

2496	roost	棲

R-2391

tree ... wife. [12]

2497	nestle	栖

R-2800

tree ... west. [10]

2498	spiny	梗

R-2447

tree ... grow late. [11]

This character refers originally to a deciduous, rough *tree* that grows on mountain plains. From this it gets the secondary sense of rugged or **spiny**.

2499	bellflower	桔

R-2519

tree ... lidded crock. [10]

2500	temple grove	杜

R-3009

tree ... soil. [7]

2501	grain rake	杷

R-2765

tree ... mosaic. [8]

2502	oar	梶

R-3120

tree ... tail. [11]

2503 R-2921	wooden pestle	杵
tree ... horse. [8]		

2504 R-2408	cane	杖
tree ... length. [7]		

2505 R-2784	sweet oak	椎
tree ... turkey. [12]		

2506 R-2539	barrel	樽
tree ... revered. [16]		

2507 R-2920	palisade	柵
tree ... tome. [9]		

2508 R-2846	turret	櫓
tree ... fish ... sun. [19]		

2509 R-3093	sturdy oak	櫨
tree ... 2 fields ... floors and ceilings. [17]		

The type of **oak** *tree* this character refers to is classically reputed to be good for making boats, carts, and the like. See FRAME 2240 for a similar right-side combination.

2510 R-2815	wooden ladle	杓
tree ... ladle. [7]		

2511 R-3087	damson	李
	tree . . . child. [7]	
2512 R-2396	raw cotton	棉
	tree . . . white . . . towel. [12]	
2513 R-2560	escutcheon	楯
	tree . . . shield. [13]	
2514 R-3130	hackberry	榎
	tree . . . summer. [14]	
2515 R-2372	birch	樺
	tree . . . splendor. [14]	
2516 R-2295	lance	槍
	tree . . . godown. [14]	
2517 R-3028	wild mulberry	柘
	tree . . . rock. [9]	
2518 R-2419	bale	梱
	tree . . . quandary. [11]	
2519 R-2631	loquat	枇
	tree . . . compare. [8]	

| 2520 | downspout | 樋 |

R-3096

tree . . . traffic. [14]

| 2521 | sled | 橇 |

R-3065

tree . . . three furs. [16]

| 2522 | enjoyment | 槃 |

R-2636

carrier . . . tree. [14]

| 2523 | bookmark | 栞 |

R-2653

two clotheslines . . . tree. [10]

| 2524 | coconut tree | 椰 |

R-2469

tree . . . ear . . . city walls. [12]

| 2525 | sandalwood | 檀 |

R-2425

tree . . . top hat . . . rotation . . . night break. [17]
Compare the right side to 壇 (1.587).

| 2526 | sumac | 樗 |

R-3006

tree . . . rain . . . ceiling . . . snare. [15]
This **sumac** (or Japanese bead tree) is a symbol for a totally useless *tree* because of its rough bark, spines, and foul-smelling leaves.

| 2527 | zelkova | 槻 |

R-2377

tree . . . standard. [15]

2528	cryptomeria	椙

R-3110

tree . . . prosperous. [12]

2529	copious	彬

R-2831

tree . . . cedar. [11]

2530	bucket	桶

R-2872

tree . . . chopseal . . . utilize. [11]

2531	ellipse	楕

R-2458

tree . . . pinnacle . . . left . . . flesh. [13]

We have met the element to the right here before, as in 惰 (1.629). The standard form for this character is actually 橢, but the abbreviation has passed into general use.

2532	star-anise	樒

R-2343

tree . . . secrecy. [15]

The **star-anise**, as you will guess from the primitive on the left, is a kind of *tree*—to be precise, a kind of Chinese evergreen that belongs to the magnolia family. It is known for its aromatic oil.

毛 FUR

2533	furball	毬

R-2319

fur . . . request. [11]

火 灬 FIRE·OVEN-FIRE

2534 R-2729	twinkle *fire . . . feathers . . . turkey.* [18]	燿
2535 R-2264	watchfire *fire . . . pup tent.* [16]	燎
2536 R-2562	torch *fire . . . gigantic.* [9]	炬
2537 R-2898	kindle *grove . . . fire.* [12]	焚
2538 R-2385	moxa *mummy . . . fire.* [7]	灸
2539 R-2939	candlelight *fire . . . net . . . bound up . . . insect.* [17] Compare the right complex of elements with 濁 (1.835).	燭
2540 R-2402	fanning *fire . . . fan.* [14]	煽
2541 R-2643	soot *fire . . . so-and-so.* [13]	煤

2542 firing	煉
R-2709	

fire . . . east. [12]
Firing here, as in the process for making bricks or refining metals.

2543 dazzling	燦
R-2856	

fire . . . wand . . . evening . . . crotch . . . rice. [17]

2544 refulgent	灼
R-2816	

fire . . . ladle. [7]

2545 branding	烙
R-2742	

fire . . . each. [10]

2546 flames	焔
R-2828	

fire . . . bound up . . . olden days. [11]
Compare right elements in 陷 (1.1315).

2547 fuse metal	熔
R-2299	

fire . . . contain. [14]
This is the character for **melt** 溶 (1.791), with the water replaced by *fire*.

2548 roast	煎
R-2616	

in front . . . oven-fire. [13]

2549 stew	烹
R-2993	

tall . . . complete . . . oven-fire. [11]

牛 COW

2550 R-2909	tug	牽
mysterious . . . crown . . . cow. [11] Write the *crown* after the first stroke of that for *mysterious*.		
2551 R-2947	female animal	牝
cow . . . spoon. [6]		
2552 R-2948	male animal	牡
cow . . . soil. [7]		

王 JEWEL

2553 R-2316	precious stone	瑶
jewel . . . condor. [13]		
2554 R-2446	chime	琳
jewel . . . grove. [12]		
2555 R-2530	marine blue	瑠
jewel . . . detain. [14]		
2556 R-2397	speckled	斑
jewel . . . plaid . . . jewel. [12]		

2557 R-2342	lapis lazuli	琉
jewel . . . infant . . . flood. [11]		
2558 R-2951	tinker with	弄
jewel . . . two hands. [7]		
2559 R-2365	burnish	瑳
jewel . . . distinction. [14]		
2560 R-2906	hone	琢
jewel . . . sow. [11]		
2561 R-2905	coral	珊
jewel . . . tome. [9]		
2562 R-2606	coral reef	瑚
jewel . . . old . . . moon. [13]		
2563 R-3066	fortunate	瑞
jewel . . . mountain . . . comb. [13]		
2564 R-2751	silicon	珪
jewel . . . ivy. [10]		
2565 R-2384	jet	玖
jewel . . . mummy. [7]		

The key word **jet** refers to the dark black lignite whose susceptibility to high polish makes it popular in ornamentation (and which also gives us the phrase "jet-black").

2566 R-2434	**crystal stone**	瑛
jewel . . . England. [12]		
2567 R-2301	**toy**	玩
jewel . . . beginning. [8]		
2568 R-2494	**tinkling**	玲
jewel . . . orders. [9]		

田 FIELD

2569 R-2588	**apprehensive**	畏
field . . . hairpin. [9]		
2570 R-3067	**lastly**	畢
field . . . siliage . . . ten. [10] The writing of this character looks more difficult than it is: 田 　 里 　 甼 　 畁 　 畁 　 畠 　 畢		
2571 R-2749	**paddy-field ridge**	畦
field . . . ivy. [11]		

疒 SICKNESS

| 2572 | itch | 痒 |

R-2757

sickness . . . sheep. [11]

| 2573 | phlegm | 痰 |

R-2781

sickness . . . inflammation. [13]

| 2574 | measles | 疹 |

R-2774

sickness . . . umbrella . . . shape. [10]

| 2575 | hemorrhoids | 痔 |

R-2715

sickness . . . temple. [11]

| 2576 | cancer | 癌 |

R-2949

sickness . . . goods . . . mountain. [17]

| 2577 | lose weight | 瘦 |

R-2382

sickness . . . monkey . . . crotch. [12]

| 2578 | scar | 痕 |

R-2705

sickness . . . silver. [11]

| 2579 | paralysis | 痺 |

R-2620

sickness . . . lowly. [13]

目 EYE

2580 R-2890	**apple of the eye**	眸
	eye . . . moo. [11]	
2581 R-2294	**dizzy**	眩
	eye . . . mysterious. [10]	
2582 R-2262	**obvious**	瞭
	eye . . . pup tent. [17]	
2583 R-2913	**eyebrow**	眉
	The *flag* here has an extra vertical stroke in it. Think of it as an **eyebrow** pencil stuck in the *eye*. [9]	

矢 ARROW

2584 R-2782	**pheasant**	雉
	arrow . . . turkey. [13]	
2585 R-2563	**carpenter's square**	矩
	arrow . . . gigantic. [10]	

石 ROCK

2586 crag R-2637 *carrier . . . rock.* [15]		磐
2587 grapnel R-2668 *rock . . . determined.* [13] Compare this stone anchor with the metal anchor 錨 in FRAME 2765.		碇
2588 blue-green R-2821 *jewel . . . white . . . rock.* [14]		碧
2589 inkstone R-2807 *rock . . . to see.* [12]		硯
2590 grindstone R-2564 *rock . . . calling card.* [10]		砥
2591 teacup R-2634 *rock . . . address.* [13] This is a **teacup** made out of *stone*. When it is made out of wood, it is written 椀 (see FRAME 2487).		碗
2592 obstacle R-2945 *rock . . . nightbreak . . . glue.* [13] Compare the right side with 得 (1.876).		碍

2593 R-3014	illustrious *rock . . . head.* [14]	碩
2594 R-2303	rocky beach *rock . . . how much.* [17]	磯
2595 R-2369	whetstone *rock . . . cliff . . . ten thousand.* [10]	砺
2596 R-3162	mill *rock . . . turkey.* [13]	碓

示 ネ ALTAR

2597 R-2401	fend off *honorable . . . altar.* [17]	禦
2598 R-3054	beseech *altar . . . longevity.* [11]	祷
2599 R-2649	ancestral tablet *altar . . . right.* [9]	祐
2600 R-2567	local god *altar . . . family name.* [8]	祇

| 2601 | ancestral shrine | 祢 |
| R-2894 | | |

altar . . . lying down . . . small. [9]

| 2602 | salarium | 禄 |
| R-2340 | | |

altar . . . broom . . . rice grains. [12]

In the same way that Roman soliders were paid in salt (hence the word **salarium**), ranking functionaries in Japan's feudal system collected their "salary" in *rice.*

| 2603 | felicitation | 禎 |
| R-2325 | | |

altar . . . upright. [13]

This kanji refers to a sign or token of congratulations.

禾 WHEAT

| 2604 | balancing scales | 秤 |
| R-3094 | | |

wheat . . . lily pad. [10]

| 2605 | millet | 黍 |
| R-3086 | | |

wheat . . . umbrella . . . grains of rice. [12]

| 2606 | bald | 禿 |
| R-2965 | | |

wheat . . . human legs. [7]

| 2607 | bear fruit | 稔 |
| R-2575 | | |

wheat . . . wish. [13]

2608 R-2623	crabgrass	稗
wheat . . . lowly. [13]		
2609 R-2258	bumper crop	穰
wheat . . . grass skirt. [18]		
2610 R-2352	imperial authority	稜
wheat . . . rice seedling . . . walking legs. [13]		
2611 R-2456	sparse	稀
wheat . . . hope. [12]		
2612 R-3004	obeisant	穆
wheat . . . spring . . . shape. [16]		

穴 HOLE

2613 R-2376	peep	窺
hole . . . protocol. [16]		
2614 R-2520	tight	窄
hole . . . saw. [10]		
2615 R-2281	cavern	窟
hole . . . yield. [13]		

2616 drill	穿
R-2944	
hole ... tusk. [9]	

2617 kitchen stove	竈
R-3068	
hole ... soil ... (bucket of) eels. [17]	

立 VASE

2618 longness	堅
R-3163	
slave ... crotch ... vase. [14]	

2619 rustling	颯
R-2527	
vase ... wind. [14]	

Note that the full character for *wind* is used here instead of the normal primitive abbreviation. The sense of the key word is the "sound of the *wind.*"

2620 outpost	站
R-3037	
vase ... fortune-telling. [10]	

2621 repose	靖
R-2247	
vase ... blue. [13]	

2622 concubine	妾
R-2904	
vase ... woman. [8]	

衤 CLOAK

2623	lapel	衿
R-2860		

cloak . . . now. [9]

2624	hem	裾
R-2389		

cloak . . . reside. [13]

2625	lined kimono	袷
R-3091		

cloak . . . fit. [11]

2626	pleated skirt	袴
R-2367		

cloak . . . St. Bernard . . . ceiling . . . snare. [11]

This kanji describes the formal divided skirt or *hakama* that you might see university students wearing at graduation. For the right side, compare 誇 (1.1244).

2627	sliding door	襖
R-2413		

cloak . . . core. [17]

This actually is the kanji for *fusuma*, an opaque sliding paper door found in Japanese houses.

竹 ⺮ BAMBOO

2628	Chinese panpipe	笙
R-2700		

bamboo . . . cell. [11]

| 2629 | raft | 筏 |

R-2329

bamboo . . . to fell. [12]

| 2630 | bamboo blinds | 簾 |

R-2642

bamboo . . . bargain. [19]

| 2631 | rattan box | 箪 |

R-2797

bamboo . . . simple. [15]

| 2632 | pole | 竿 |

R-2652

bamboo . . . clothesline. [9]

| 2633 | spatula | 箆 |

R-2570

bamboo . . . hood . . . umbrella . . . compare. [14]

| 2634 | foil | 箔 |

R-2245

bamboo . . . overnight. [14]

| 2635 | wardrobe | 笥 |

R-2254

bamboo . . . director. [11]

The term here refers to what contains one's robes, not the robes themselves.

| 2636 | arrow shaft | 箭 |

R-2617

bamboo . . . in front. [15]

| 2637 | ancient harp | 筑 |

R-2410

bamboo . . . craft . . . mediocre. [12]

This **ancient harp**, a predecessor of the present Japanese koto, had 5, 13, or 21 strings.

2638 R-2868	cage	篭

bamboo . . . dragon. [16]

2639 R-3164	slender bamboo	篠

bamboo . . . person . . . walking stick . . . taskmaster . . . tree. [17]

2640 R-3092	chopsticks	箸

bamboo . . . puppet. [14]

2641 R-2420	redaction	纂

bamboo . . . eyeball . . . St. Bernard . . . thread. [20]

2642 R-2847	bamboo cane	竺

bamboo . . . two. [8]

2643 R-2663	winnowing fan	箕

bamboo . . . bushel basket. [14]

2644 R-2272	backpack	笈

bamboo . . . reach out. [9]

2645 R-2270	livraison	篇

bamboo . . . door . . . scrapbooks. [15]

The French word captures better than any English word can the range of uses this character has in designating chapter, volume, part, or fascicle of a classical text.

2646 **should**		筈
R-2711		

bamboo . . . tongue. [12]

The sense of the key word here is not one of moral obligation (as we saw in 莫, FRAME 2105) but rather of something that is "expected" of one.

2647 **winnow**		簸
R-2722		

bamboo . . . bushel basket . . . pelt. [19]

米 RICE

2648 **settlings**		粕
R-2246		

rice . . . white. [11]

The key word here refers to the sediment left in making rice saké. Its meaning is substantially the same as the character in the following frame.

2649 **lees**		糟
R-2260		

rice . . . cadet. [17]

2650 **paste**		糊
R-2604		

rice . . . old . . . moon. [15]

2651 **unhulled rice**		籽
R-3100		

rice . . . blade. [9]

2652 rice bran R-2437 *rice . . . ease.* [17]		糠
2653 excrement R-2986 *rice . . . uncommon.* [17]		糞
2654 foxtail millet R-2903 *Old West . . . rice.* [12]		粟

糸 THREAD

2655 link up R-2874 *car . . . missile . . . thread.* [17]		繫
2656 twine R-2521 *thread . . . meeting . . . scrapbooks.* [14] The key word here is meant to indicate woven cord.		綸
2657 carpet yarn R-2851 *thread . . . ten . . . fiesta.* [12]		絨
2658 ties R-2259 *thread . . . half.* [11] The sense of the key word is as in the phrase "family **ties**."		絆

| 2659 | scarlet | 緋 |
| R-2718 | | |

thread . . . un-. [14]

| 2660 | synthesis | 綜 |
| R-2825 | | |

thread . . . religion. [14]

| 2661 | string | 紐 |
| R-2455 | | |

thread . . . sign of the cow. [10]

| 2662 | chinstrap | 紘 |
| R-2614 | | |

thread . . . by his side . . . elbow. [10]

| 2663 | summarize | 纏 |
| R-3010 | | |

thread . . . cave . . . computer . . . animal legs . . . earth . [21]

| 2664 | gorgeous | 絢 |
| R-2581 | | |

thread . . . decameron. [12]

| 2665 | embroidery | 繡 |
| R-2917 | | |

thread . . . solemn. [17]

| 2666 | pongee | 紬 |
| R-2777 | | |

thread . . . sprout. [11]

| 2667 | ornate | 綺 |
| R-2541 | | |

thread . . . strange. [14]

2668 R-2355	damask	綾

thread . . . rice seedlings . . . walking legs. [14]

2669 R-2292	catgut	絃

thread . . . mysterious. [11]

The sense of the key word is that of "strings" used for stringed instruments, which are not necessarily the intestines of cats.

2670 R-2669	come apart at the seams	綻

thread . . . determine. [14]

2671 R-3123	stripe	縞

thread . . . tall. [16]

2672 R-2326	gimp	綬

thread . . . accept. [14]

The key word here refers to wound yarn with a hard core.

2673 R-2853	gossamer	紗

thread . . . few. [10]

舟 BOAT

2674 R-2592	rudder	舵

boat . . . house . . . spoon. [11]

2675 R-2293	gunwale	舷

boat . . . mysterious. [11]

耳 EAR

2676 R-2823	strung together	聯

ear . . . two cocoons . . . cactus. [17]

The last primitive, cactus, does not appear elsewhere in this book, but is useful to learn, especially for writing old forms. It is pictographic.

2677 R-2339	attentive	聡

ear . . . public . . . heart. [14]

2678 R-3069	summons	聘

ear . . . sprout . . . snare. [10]

2679 R-2916	addiction	耽

ear . . . crown . . . human legs. [10]

2680 R-2467	exclamation	耶

ear . . . city walls. [8]

The key word here was used classically for general **exclamation**.

虫 INSECT

2681 flea R-2381 *crotch . . . two drops . . . insect.* [10]		蚤
2682 crab R-2416 *unravel . . . insect.* [19]		蟹
2683 protein R-2950 *zoo . . . insect.* [11]		蛋
2684 hibernation R-3030 *tenacious . . . insect.* [17]		蟄
2685 housefly R-3118 *insect . . . eels.* [15]		蠅
2686 ant R-2257 *insect . . . righteousness.* [19]		蟻
2687 bee R-2284 *insect . . . walking legs . . . bushes.* [13]		蜂
2688 wax R-2943 *insect . . . owl . . . wind . . . corncob.* [14] Compare the right side to 猟 (1.1940).		蝋

| 2689 | shrimp | 蝦 |
| R-2374 | | |

insect ... staples ... mouth ... box ... crotch. [15]
Compare the right side with 暇 (1.1882).

| 2690 | octopus | 蛸 |
| R-3165 | | |

insect ... candle. [13]

| 2691 | screw | 螺 |
| R-2919 | | |

insect ... accumulate. [17]

| 2692 | cicada | 蝉 |
| R-2810 | | |

insect ... simple. [15]

| 2693 | frog | 蛙 |
| R-2752 | | |

insect ... ivy. [12]

| 2694 | moth | 蛾 |
| R-2288 | | |

insect ... ego. [13]

| 2695 | clam | 蛤 |
| R-3121 | | |

insect ... fit. [12]

| 2696 | leech | 蛭 |
| R-3166 | | |

insect ... climax. [12]

| 2697 | oyster | 蛎 |
| R-2368 | | |

insect ... cliff ... ten thousand. [11]

罒 NET

2698 ruled lines R-2956 *net . . . ivy . . . wand.* [14]		罫
2699 insult R-2845 *net . . . horse.* [15]		罵

衣 CLOTHES

2700 stole R-2691 *add . . . clothes.* [11] This key word is used for the **stole** of a Buddhist monk, generally in combination with the character in the following frame.		袈
2701 monk's sash R-2453 *water . . . few . . . clothes.* [13] See note in previous frame.		裟

弋 THANKSGIVING

2702 accept humbly R-2697 *Thanksgiving . . . uncommon.* [17]		戴

| 2703　incision R-2696 | 截 |

Thanksgiving . . . turkey. [14]

| 2704　I wonder R-2695 | 哉 |

plantation . . . mouth. [9]

The sense of the key word is as in sentences such as "**I wonder** when it will arrive." The character, however, is used now only in poetry and names.

言 WORDS

| 2705　counsel R-2579 | 詢 |

words . . . decameron. [13]

| 2706　polite R-3070 | 諄 |

words . . . receive. [15]

| 2707　vendetta R-2979 | 讐 |

two turkeys . . . words. [23]

| 2708　remonstrate R-2710 | 諫 |

words . . . east. [15]

| 2709　riddle R-3095 | 謎 |

words . . . astray. [16]

2710 R-2746	verify	諒	
	words ... capital. [15]		
2711 R-2421	compliment	讃	
	words ... approval. [22]		
2712 R-2786	who	誰	
	words ... turkey. [15]		
2713 R-2438	query	訊	
	words ... ten ... fishhook. [10]		
2714 R-2531	split up	訣	
	words ... guillotine. [11]		
2715 R-2543	visit a shrine	詣	
	words ... delicious. [13]		
2716 R-2311	give up	諦	
	words ... sovereign. [16]		
2717 R-2576	elucidate	詮	
	words ... complete. [13]		
2718 R-2594	prevarication	詫	
	words ... house ... spoon. [12]		

2719 R-2418	familiarity	誼
words ... best regards. [15]		
2720 R-2776	fallible	謬
words ... feathers ... umbrella ... shape. [18]		
2721 R-3167	beg pardon	詫
words ... home. [13]		
2722 R-3071	advise	諏
words ... take. [15]		
2723 R-3023	proverb	諺
words ... lad. [16]		
2724 R-2719	slander	誹
words ... un-. [15]		
2725 R-2414	so-called	謂
words ... stomach. [17]		
2726 R-2508	secret agent	諜
words ... generations ... tree. [17]		
2727 R-2761	footnote	註
words ... candlestick. [12]		

| 2728 | parable | 譬 |

R-2625

ketchup . . . words. [20]

車 CAR

| 2729 | rumble | 轟 |

R-2972

three cars. [21]

| 2730 | reinforce | 輔 |

R-2681

car . . . dog tag. [14]

| 2731 | spoke | 輻 |

R-2703

car . . . wealth. [16]

The key word refers to the **spoke** of a wheel.

| 2732 | assemble | 輯 |

R-2590

car . . . mouth . . . ear. [16]

豸 BADGER

| 2733 | countenance | 貌 |

R-3002

badger . . . white . . . human legs. [14]

2734 panther R-2859	豹
badger ... ladle. [10]	

貝 SHELL

2735 despicable R-2660	賤
shell ... fiesta. [13]	
2736 affix R-2877	貼
shell ... fortuneteller. [12]	
2737 get R-3124	貰
generation ... shell. [12]	
2738 graft R-2743	賂
shells ... each. [13]	
2739 bustling R-2511	賑
shells ... sign of the dragon. [14]	

𧾷 WOODEN LEG

2740 stumble R-3034	蹟
wooden leg ... substance. [22]	

2741 R-2312	hoof	蹄
wooden leg . . . sovereign. [16]		
2742 R-2362	kick	蹴
wooden leg . . . concerning. [19]		
2743 R-2548	vestiges	蹟
wooden leg . . . blame. [18]		
2744 R-2366	straddle	跨
wooden leg . . . St. Bernard . . . ceiling . . . snare. [13]		
2745 R-2552	kneel	跪
wooden leg . . . danger [13]		

酉 WHISKY

2746 R-2324	soy sauce	醬
leader . . . whisky bottle. [17]		
2747 R-2840	whey	醍
whisky bottle . . . just so. [16]		
2748 R-2901	hooch	酊
whisky bottle . . . glue. [10]		
This kanji is used for thick saké, made from various kinds of grains.		

| 2749 | ghee | 醐 |

R-2607

whisky bottle . . . old . . . moon. [16]

| 2750 | awakening | 醒 |

R-2698

whisky bottle . . . star. [16]

| 2751 | strong saké | 醇 |

R-2675

whisky bottle . . . receive. [15]

麦_ BARLEY

| 2752 | noodles | 麺 |

R-2395

barley . . . mask. [16]

| 2753 | malt | 麹 |

R-2361

barley . . . bound up . . . rice. [15]

金 METAL

| 2754 | button | 釦 |

R-2812

metal . . . mouth. [11]

| 2755 | keg | 銚 |

R-2645

metal . . . portent. [14]

2756 plow R-2428		鋤

metal . . . help. [15]

This is the **plow** whose *metal* blades were used to grill meat and which gives us the word *sukiyaki* (**plow**-fried).

2757 pot R-3168		鍋

metal . . . jawbone. [17]

2758 arrowhead R-2252		鏑

metal . . . antique. [19]

2759 handsaw R-2388		鋸

metal . . . reside. [16]

2760 awl R-2785		錐

metal . . . turkey. [16]

2761 key R-2327		鍵

metal . . . build. [17]

2762 hoe R-2307		鍬

metal . . . autumn. [17]

2763 rivet R-3102		鋲

metal . . . soldier. [15]

2764 tin R-2957		錫

metal . . . piggy bank. [16]

| 2765 | anchor | 錨 |

R-2275

metal ... seedlings. [16]

| 2766 | nail | 釘 |

R-2707

metal ... spike. [10]

| 2767 | javelin | 鑓 |

R-3169

metal ... dispatch. [21]

| 2768 | sword's point | 鋒 |

R-2285

metal ... walking legs ... bushes. [15]

| 2769 | hammer | 鎚 |

R-2387

metal ... chase after. [17]

Compare the **wooden hammer** 槌 in FRAME 2477.

| 2770 | carillion | 鉦 |

R-2644

metal ... correct. [13]

This character indicates a Western bell, which is struck from the inside by a gong, unlike the oriental bell 鐘, which is struck from the outside.

| 2771 | rust | 錆 |

R-2248

metal ... blue. [16]

Since Chinese and Japanese distinguish *blue* and green differently from European languages, it is not surprising that the verdigris that occurs on copper is here indicated by the element for *blue*.

2772 R-2883	cluster	鍾
metal . . . heavy. [17]		

2773 R-3170	scissors	鋏
metal . . . St. Bernard dog . . . assembly line. [15] This is the character on which the element for *scissors* 夾 was based.		

門 GATES

2774 R-2985	flash	閃
gates . . . person. [10]		

2775 R-2977	agony	悶
gates . . . heart. [12]		

2776 R-2666	side gate	閤
gates . . . fit. [14]		

2777 R-2714	pitch dark	闇
gates . . . sound. [17]		

雫 WEATHER

2778 R-3171	**trickle**	雫
weather . . . below. [11]		
2779 R-2375	**haze**	霞
weather . . . hobby. [17]		

卓 MIST

2780 R-2834	**quill**	翰
mist . . . umbrella . . . feathers. [16]		
2781 R-2803	**auspices**	斡
mist . . . umbrella . . . Big Dipper. [14]		

革 LEATHER

2782 R-2290	**saddle**	鞍
leather . . . relax. [15]		
2783 R-2448	**whip**	鞭
leather . . . convenience. [18]		

2784	saddle straps	鞘
R-2626		
leather . . . candle. [16]		

2785	briefcase	鞄
R-3097		
leather . . . wrap. [14]		

2786	pliable	靭
R-2489		
leather . . . blade. [12]		

2787	terminate	鞠
R-2360		
leather . . . bound up . . . rice. [17]		

頁 HEAD

2788	immediate	頓
R-2611		
earthworm . . . head. [13]		

2789	overturn	顛
R-2693		
true . . . head. [19]		

2790	brush tip	穎
R-2999		
spoon . . . wheat . . . head. [16]		

2791	about that time	頃
R-2422		
spoon . . . head. [11]		

| 2792 cheek | 頰 |
| R-2266 | |

scissors . . . head. [15]

| 2793 exceedingly | 頗 |
| R-2721 | |

pelt . . . head. [14]

| 2794 accolade | 頌 |
| R-2819 | |

public . . . head. [13]

| 2795 chin | 顎 |
| R-2475 | |

two mouths . . . ceiling . . . snare . . . head. [18]

| 2796 neck and throat | 頸 |
| R-2523 | |

spool . . . head. [14]

The key word here is meant to specify the anatomical **neck**, to distinguish it from the broader uses of the character 首 (1.70).

食 食 FOOD

| 2797 feed | 餌 |
| R-2811 | |

food . . . ear. [14]

The sense of the key word here is that of bait or **feed** for animals.

| 2798 repast | 餐 |
| R-3012 | |

wand . . . evening . . . crotch . . . food. [16]

2799 feast R-2332	饗

hometown . . . food. [20]
The **feast** intended here is a banquet of food.

2800 eclipse R-2838	蝕

eat . . . insect. [14]

2801 sweets R-3090	飴

food . . . pedestal. [13]

2802 mochi R-2514	餅

food . . . puzzle. [14]
Mochi is the glutinous rice the Japanese pound into cakes.

馬 TEAM OF HORSES

2803 stretcher R-2690	駕

add . . . team of horses. [15]

2804 piebald R-2998	驊

horse . . . simple. [19]

2805 rush R-2772	馳

team of horses . . . scorpion. [13]

2806 R-2269	cheat	騙
team of horses . . . door . . . scrapbook. [19]		

2807 R-2809	tame	馴
team of horses . . . stream. [13]		

2808 R-2886	rebuttal	駁
team of horses . . . two sheaves. [14]		

2809 R-3072	gallop	駈
team of horses . . . hill. [15]		

2810 R-3073	donkey	驢
team of horses . . . tiger . . . field . . . dish. [26]		

魚 FISH

2811 R-2346	eel	鰻
fish . . . mandala. [22]		

2812 R-2767	sea bream	鯛
fish . . . circumference. [19]		

2813 R-3099	sardine	鰯
fish . . . weak. [21]		

2814	trout	鱒
R-2540		
fish ... revered. [23]		

2815	salmon	鮭
R-2750		
fish ... ivy. [17]		

2816	tuna	鮪
R-3133		
fish ... possession. [17]		

2817	sweet smelt	鮎
R-2880		
fish ... fortune-telling. [16]		

2818	horse mackerel	鯵
R-3115		
fish ... nonplussed. [19]		

2819	cod	鱈
R-3132		
fish ... snow. [22]		

2820	mackerel	鯖
R-3182		
fish ... blue. [19]		

2821	shark	鮫
R-3129		
fish ... mingle. [17]		

2822	bonito	鰹
R-3127		
fish ... strict. [23]		

| 2823 | bullhead | 鰍 |

R-3172

fish . . . autumn. [20]

| 2824 | alligator | 鰐 |

R-2476

fish . . . two mouths . . . ceiling . . . snare. [20]

| 2825 | crucian carp | 鮒 |

R-3134

fish . . . adhere to. [16]

| 2826 | sushi | 鮨 |

R-3173

fish . . . delicious [17]

| 2827 | fish fin | 鰭 |

R-3075

fish . . . old man . . . sun. [21]

鳥 BIRD

| 2828 | seagull | 鴎 |

R-2713

ward . . . bird. [15]

| 2829 | roc | 鵬 |

R-2277

companion . . . bird. [19]

| 2830 | parakeet | 鸚 |

R-3076

suckling babe . . . bird. [19]

This character is generally used in combination with that in the following frame. See FRAME 2193 for the element to the left.

2831 R-2817	parrot	鸚
warrior . . . bird. [19]		
2832 R-3174	cormorant	鵜
younger brother . . . bird. [18]		
2833 R-2297	heron	鷺
path . . . bird. [24]		
2834 R-2363	eagle	鷲
concerning . . . bird. [23]		
2835 R-3077	wild duck	鴨
push . . . bird. [16]		
2836 R-3074	black kite	鳶
arrow . . . bird. [14]		
2837 R-3044	owl	梟
bird . . . tree. [11]		
Note that the "tail feathers" of the *bird* disappear (or are replaced by) the *tree*. This is the only occasion in the kanji in which the element for *bird* is so altered.		

鹿 DEER

2838 R-2958	dust *deer . . . soil.* [14]	塵
2839 R-2371	foot of a mountain *grove . . . deer.* [19]	麓
2840 R-2664	giraffe *deer . . . bushel basket.* [19]	麒

CHAPTER 3

Miscellaneous Kanji

THE CHARACTERS introduced in this chapter (107 in all) are not arranged in any particular order, except where one serves as an element for the next.

2841	Hades	冥

R-2470

crown ... sun ... six. [10]

The reference here is to the underworld, the world of the dead. By way of the classic Greek association, it is also used for the planet Pluto.

2842	close the eyes	瞑

R-2471

eye ... Hades. [15]

2843	murky	暝

R-2472

sun ... Hades. [14]

2844	sitting in meditation	坐

R-2356

assembly line ... soil. [7]

2845	sprain	挫

R-2357

fingers ... sitting in meditation. [10]

2846	first day of the month	朔

R-2572

mountain goat ... moon. [10]

2847 go upstream
R-2573

遡

first day of the month . . . road. [13]

2848 drag
R-2479

曳

sun . . . under one's arm. [6]

Take particular care not to confuse this key word with the familiar primitive element for drag ⌐.

2849 dribble out
R-2480

洩

water . . . drag. [9]

2850 comet
R-2891

彗

two bushes . . . broom. [11]

2851 astute
R-2893

慧

comet . . . heart. [15]

Note that the second stroke on the element for *broom* does not pass through as it does in the character for *comet*. A similar change takes place in the character 急. It would be nice if it were possible to make a rule for this kind of transformation, but the evolution of the kanji has not been consistent on this point.

2852 applaud
R-2686

嘉

drum . . . add. [14]

2853 evil
R-2449

兇

villain . . . human legs. [6]

2854 helmet
R-3078

white bird between *two open boxes . . . human legs.* [11]

兜

2855 bracing
R-2857

St. Bernard with *two pairs of sheaves* on each side. [11]
The sense of the key word is of something refreshing and invigorating.

爽

2856 depressed
R-2936

two sheaves in a *woods . . . net . . . silver . . . glue.* [22]
The key word here refers to the psychological state of depression.

欝

2857 kalpa
R-2865

gone . . . muscles. [7]
A **kalpa** is a mythical measure of time (something over 4 billion years) used in ancient India and today mainly in classic Buddhist texts.

劫

2858 erection
R-3079

needle . . . crown . . . child . . . muscles. [9]

勃

2859 bemoan
R-2796

strawman . . . yawn. [15]

歎

2860 palanquin
R-3027

Think of this character as entertainment with a car since the only difference between it and the character for entertainment is the substitution of the element for *car* in place of *same.* [17]

輿

| 2861 | southeast | 巽 |

R-2359

two snakes . . . strung together. [12]

One of the directions in classical Chinese geomancy, this character is used in Japanese today chiefly in names.

| 2862 | warped | 歪 |

R-2897

negation . . . correct. [9]

| 2863 | jade green | 翠 |

R-3050

feathers . . . graduate. [14]

| 2864 | blue-black | 黛 |

R-2278

substitute . . . black. [16]

| 2865 | tripod | 鼎 |

R-2963

This character is not hard to remember if you think of it as back-to-back characters for *one-sided* with a *sun* in the middle (and necessitating a shorter vertical stroke for *one-sided*). [12]

| 2866 | rocksalt | 鹵 |

R-2991

wand . . . pent up . . . sheave . . . four dots. [11]

| 2867 | lye | 鹼 |

R-2251

rocksalt . . . awl. [19]

| 2868 | reserved | 虔 |

R-3139

tiger . . . plaid. [10]

2869 swallow
R-2983

twenty... two people back to back... mouth... oven-fire.
The **swallow** referred to here is the bird. [16]

燕

2870 lick
R-2780

outhouse... delicious. [14]

嘗

2871 almost
R-2655

bones... pedestal. [9]

殆

2872 start
R-2392

child... dish. [8]

孟

2873 mahjong tiles
R-2622

one-sided... lowly. [12]

牌

2874 remains
R-2769

skeleton... acorn. [16]

骸

2875 peek
R-3175

director... see. [12]

覗

2876 mottled
R-3080

tiger... form. [11]

彪

2877 Manchu dynasty
R-2483

bonsai... wheat. [10]

秦

| 2878 | sparrow | 雀 |

R-2858

few ... turkey. [11]

The last stroke of *few* doubles up with the first stroke of *turkey*.

| 2879 | peregrine falcon | 隼 |

R-2426

turkey ... needle. [10]

| 2880 | shimmering | 耀 |

R-2728

ray of light ... feathers ... turkey. [20]

| 2881 | *ebisu* | 夷 |

R-2990

great ... bow. [6]

Ebisu is a Japanization of the Ainu word *enchu* which means "person." In former times, it was used to mean any of the "uncivilized" people living north of the area of present-day Tokyo.

| 2882 | relatives | 戚 |

R-2961

uncle ... parade. [11]

| 2883 | cyst | 囊 |

R-2881

needle ... middle ... crown ... eight ... celery ... scarf. [19]

Note how the elements for *needle* and *middle* share a common, vertical stroke in this particularly complex character.

| 2884 | domburi | 丼 |

R-3081

well ... drop. [5]

| 2885 | carefree | 暢 |

R-2732

monkey ... piggy bank. [14]

| 2886 | circling | 廻 |

R-2791

stretch . . . -times. [9]

| 2887 | capital suburbs | 畿 |

R-2304

two cocoons . . . field . . . fiesta. [15]

| 2888 | elation | 欣 |

R-2854

ax . . . yawn. [8]

| 2889 | stalwart | 毅 |

R-2899

vase . . . sow . . . missile. [15]

| 2890 | this | 斯 |

R-3016

bushel basket . . . axe. [12]

This character is not substantially different from the character we identified as **this here** 此 (FRAME 2043).

| 2891 | wooden spoon | 匙 |

R-2849

just so . . . spoon. [11]

The character for **spoon** already learned 匕 (1.444) is actually an abbreviation of this fuller character. The meanings are essentially the same.

| 2892 | set straight | 匡 |

R-3003

box . . . king. [6]

| 2893 | founding | 肇 |

R-3005

door . . . taskmaster . . . brush. [14]

You will recognize the combination at the top here from the character 啓 (1.1085).

2894   Utamaro

R-3116

    麿

hemp . . . spine. [18]

This kanji was used during the Heian period to refer to oneself. It is a home-grown Japanese character whose reading まろ comes from combining the Chinese readings of its two elements. It is used today only for names, the most famous of which is the name of the celebrated painter of *ukiyo-e* paintings, **Utamaro** 歌麿.

2895   conglomerate

R-2882

    叢

upside down in a row . . . soil . . . take. [18]

This character is often used for collections of books or essays; the only reason for the choice of the key word is that the number of synonyms for "collection" has been fairly exhausted already!

2896   entreat

R-3013

    宥

sheaf . . . possess. [8]

2897   symmetrically patterned

R-2717

    斐

un- . . . plaid. [12]

2898   magistrate

R-2887

    卿

silver in the middle of . . . the sign of the hare. [12]

2899   fiddle with

R-2302

    翫

learn . . . beginning. [15]

2900   within

R-2837

    於

compass . . . umbrella . . . two drops. [8]

| 2901 | hackneyed | 套 |
| R-2911 | | |

St. Bernard . . . hair. [10]

| 2902 | rebellion | 叛 |
| R-2658 | | |

half . . . . . . anti-. [9]

| 2903 | sharp point | 尖 |
| R-2827 | | |

a small tip on something... large. [6]

| 2904 | crock | 壺 |
| R-2937 | | |

samurai . . . crown . . . Asia. [11]

Note how the second stroke in *crown* doubles up with the first stroke of *Asia.*

| 2905 | sapience | 叡 |
| R-2932 | | |

wand . . . crown . . . ceiling . . . valley with eye (instead of mouth) . . . crotch. [16]

In order to remember the change in the element for *valley,* think of the clear-seeing *eye* that distinguishes homo sapiens.

| 2906 | chieftain | 酋 |
| R-2938 | | |

horns . . . whisky bottle. [9]

| 2907 | nightingale | 鴬 |
| R-3000 | | |

schoolhouse . . . bird. [16]

| 2908 | incandescent | 赫 |
| R-2412 | | |

two reds. [14]

| 2909 | supinate | 臥 |

R-2974

slave . . . person. [9]

The somewhat archaic-sounding key word here indicates someone streched out or lying flat.

| 2910 | nephew | 甥 |

R-2699

cell . . . male. [12]

| 2911 | gourd | 瓢 |

R-2274

ballot . . . melon. [16]

| 2912 | biwa | 琵 |

R-2632

two jewels . . . this here. [12]

This character is usually found with the next one, to give the **biwa**, a Japanese lute.

| 2913 | lute | 琶 |

R-2763

two jewels . . . mosaic. [12]

| 2914 | forked | 叉 |

R-2971

crotch . . . drop. [3]

This character, incidentally, is used in the word for "tuning **fork**."

| 2915 | rose of Sharon | 舜 |

R-2440

birdhouse . . . sunglasses. [12]

| 2916 | dry field | 畠 |

R-3176

dove . . . field. [10]

2917 fist	拳
R-3082	
quarter . . . hand. [10]	

2918 vegetable patch	圃
R-2684	
pent in . . . dog tag. [10]	

2919 helping hand	丞
R-2394	
complete . . . water . . . floor. [6]	
The shape of this character is already familiar from the character 蒸 (1.1900). As we learned then, the second stroke of *complete* doubles up with the first stroke for *water*.	

2920 translucent	亮
R-2907	
tall . . . crown . . . human legs. [9]	

2921 blood relative	胤
R-2989	
human legs surrounding a *cocoon* and *flesh.* [9]	

2922 transcription	疏
R-2836	
zoo . . . infant . . . flood. [12]	

2923 ointment	膏
R-2557	
tall . . . flesh. [14]	
Note how the element *tall* is compressed in order to fit on top.	

2924 pioneer	魁
R-3026	
ghost . . . Big Dipper. [14]	

2925 ambrosial R-2431		馨
voice ... missile ... incense. [20]		
2926 label R-2507		牒
one-sided ... generation ... tree. [13]		
2927 glimpse R-2321		瞥
shredder ... eye. [17]		
2928 large hill R-2481		阜
maestro ... needle. [8]		
This is the original character that was abbreviated to form the element we learned as *pinnacle* ß .		
2929 testicle R-2462		睾
blood ... happiness. [14]		
2930 sorceress R-3040		巫
craft ... assembly line. [7]		
2931 empathetic R-2677		敦
receive ... taskmaster. [12]		
2932 Andromeda R-2748		奎
St. Bernard ... ivy. [9]		
2933 soar R-3048		翔
sheep ... wings. [12]		

2934 beaming
R-2702

皓

white ... revelation. [12]

2935 tenebrous
R-3083

黎

wheat ... (slip)knot ... umbrella ... rice grains. [15]

Take special care in writing the second element here. You might think of it as a "slip*knot*" (in which one stroke has slipped off).

2936 bold
R-2867

赳

run ... cornucopia. [10]

2937 stop short
R-3029

巳

This character can be kept distinct from the familiar sign of the *snake* 巳 (1.2042) by noting that the final stroke **stops short**. [3]

2938 thornbush
R-3033

棘

This character is no different in meaning from the character already learned for **thorn** 刺 (1.417). The only difference in writing is the repetition of the element composed of tree and belt. (Incidentally, that element on its own 束 has the same meaning of **thorn**, though it is far less commonly seen.) [12]

2939 crowd
R-3038

聚

ear ... crotch ... two drops ... person ... rag. [14]

This character should not be confused with 衆 (1.1857). Despite the similarity, it is neither an abbreviated nor an alternate form of it. If anything, in modern usage it is most likely to be replaced with 集 (1.559).

2940 resucitate
R-2701

甦

grow late ... cell. [12]

2941 pruning <small>R-2618</small> *in front . . . dagger.* [11]	剪
2942 upbringing <small>R-3177</small> *somebody . . . beautiful.* [16]	躾
2943 plentiful <small>R-2515</small> *fruit . . . many.* [14]	夥
2944 snore <small>R-2650</small> *nose . . . dry.* [17]	鼾
2945 cast a spell <small>R-3178</small> *exit . . . altar.* [19]	祟

CHAPTER 4

Western Measurements

THE HANDFUL of characters presented in this chapter are meant to introduce you to the basic principles used in writing Western units of measurement. Contemporary Japanese has by and large discarded this way of writing, but it is not uncommon to meet these characters in historical texts. As frightening as they might appear at first, there is a very clear logic to their composition.

2946   kilometer
R-3101

糎

rice ... one thousand. [9]

The character 米 is used for **meter** (from the sound). Thus, a **kilometer** is made by adding the element for thousand.

2947   centimeter
R-3108

糎

rice ... one rin. [15]

The reason that the *rin* (1.178) or 1/1000th of a yen is added to the meter to give us **centimeter** is that 厘 originally meant 1/100th, and 毛 1/1000th, as we see in the following frame.

2948   millimeter
R-3179

粍

rice ... fur. [10]

Incidentally, you should note that the same conventions are used to create litres, centilitres, and millilitres, based on another kanji chosen for its sound: 立, 竏, and 竓.

2949   ton
R-2612

噸

mouth ... immediate. [16]

The character 頓, again from the sound, gives us a start to that for a **ton**. The addition of the element of mouth to the left indicates that it is used for its sound and to convey a meaning other than the normal meaning of the character. This is a device commonly used in written Chinese.

2950   mile
R-2601

哩

mouth ... one ri. [10]

Although the **mile** is longer than the *ri*, the two are close enough that the addition of the mouth can indicate a foreign unit of measurement.

2951   nautical mile
R-2599

浬

water ... one ri. [10]

Since the Japanese did not have a separate unit for measuring nautical *ri*, this character was used for the Western measurement of the **nautical mile**. The same holds true of the characters in the next two frames.

2952   inch
R-3180

吋

mouth ... glue. [6]

2953   foot
R-3181

呎

mouth ... shaku. [6]

CHAPTER 5

Phonetic Characters

WHILE THE *kana* syllabaries have taken over most of the chores of incorporating loan words in their original sounds, a few exceptions have survived. The following group of characters are used mainly today for their sound value, rather than for their meaning. In each case, the sound is provided by a signal primitive, as will be indicated in Part Two of this volume. For now, the signal primitive (or its composite elements) have been <u>underlined</u>.

2954 brahman
R-2544

梵

This is the sound character for the Sanskrit word **brahman**, and is also used to indicate the Sanskrit language as such. Its elements are grove ... <u>mediocre</u>. [11]

2955 Shakyamuni Buddha
R-2593

陀

pinnacle ... <u>house</u> ... <u>spoon</u>. [7]

This character, originally meaning "precipitous" (roughly the same as the character of that key word already learned 險 (1.1672), is now used chiefly for its sound. It forms part of the transliteration of the name of the **Buddha**; hence the key word.

2956 bodhisattva
R-2976

薩

flowers ... pinnacle ... <u>products</u>. [16]

Although this character can be used as an abbreviation of **bodhisattva**, the full writing combines it with that in the following frame. Both of them are transliterations of Sanskrit terms.

2957 bo tree
R-2896

菩

flowers ... <u>vase</u> ... <u>mouth</u>. [11]

2958 babble
R-2415

唖

mouth ... Asia. [10]

The sense of the key word is that of a baby oohing and aahing.

2959 Sanskrit ka
R-2688

迦

add ... road. [8]

This kanji is used to represent the sound "ka" when transcribing words from Sanskrit.

2960 interrogative
R-2997

那

sword ... two ... city walls. [7]

Used classically to indicate an **interrogative** part of speech, this character is used chiefly now for its sound.

2961 moo
R-2889

牟

elbow ... cow. [6]

This is the character classically used for the sound that a *cow* makes.

These final two characters, taken together, are the Chinese phonetic transliterations of the English word *coffee*, which is the principal form in which you are likely to meet them today. The key words, however, are drawn from their classical meanings.

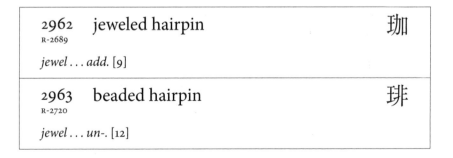

2962 jeweled hairpin
R-2689

珈

jewel ... add. [9]

2963 beaded hairpin
R-2720

琲

jewel ... un-. [12]

CHAPTER 6

Old and Alternate Forms

EARLIER ON, in FRAME 2352 of chapter 2, we introduced an old form of the character for technique (芸→ 藝). In this chapter we pick up 37 more old and alternate forms. In some cases, the older form has never been "updated." In others, both forms are still in use.

Examples of other cases where older forms and newer abbreviations occur are given in their respective frames.

2964   Japanese cypress [old]
R-3190

tree ... umbrella ... one ... pent-in ... small ... sun. [11]

The right side of this character looks rather more formidable than it is. The tricky part lies in the elements that have been described as *"pent-in ... small."* (The latter element you will remember from the element for *outhouse* 峃 or *candle* 肖.) The combination, when it appears in other characters, is generally abbreviated to the shape of the element for sun. In any case, drawing the shape will show it to be quite natural. Here are some examples of the old form and their standard, simpler forms:

OLD FORM	MODERN ABBREVIATION
會	会 (1.752)
繪	絵 (1.1346)

2965   bridle's bit   繅
R-3112   口

thread ... cart ... thread ... mouth. [22]

The primitive at the top of this character is abbreviated in more common words as 亦, a primitive element that was learned in VOL. 1 (page 359). Note the following examples:

OLD FORM	MODERN ABBREVIATION
變	変 (1.1745)
戀	恋 (1.1748)

灣   湾 (1.1749)

2966   abyss [old]

R-3199

淵

On the left is the *water* and on the right a combination of the character for *one-sided* and its mirror image joined by a single stroke. Think of it as a hanging rope-bridge strung perilously across the **abyss**. [12]

    The newer form for this character is 渊, which was learned above in FRAME 2325.

2967   v

R-3195

伍

person . . . five. [6]

This character, originally meaning a group of 5 persons, is now used as an alternate form of the character 五, mainly in official documents.

2968   x

R-3194

什

person . . . ten. [4]

As in the previous frame, this character is an alternative form for 十.

2969   ten thousand [old]

R-2725

萬

flower . . . Talking Cricket. [18]

This is also used in documents, but is more common as a character in its own right. When it appears as a primitive forming a part of other characters, it is normally abbreviated to the form 万. In addition to the new character in the following frame, note the following examples:

OLD FORM	MODERN ABBREVIATION
蠣	蛎 (2.2967)
勵	(1.866)

2970   pass through

R-2726

邁

ten thousand . . . road. [16]

The "old" element in this character is that for road, which has an extra initial stroke. See also the following frame.

2971 tough 逞
R-2341

display . . . road. [11]

Note that, as in the previous frame, the element for *road* has an extra stroke generally omitted in more common characters. When writing this character, it is not incorrect to use the standard form of the primitive element.

2972 lamp [old] 燈
R-3191

fire . . . ascend. [16]

The primitive at the right of this character is generally, though not always, abbreviated today as 灯 (1.165). The older form of the primitive to the right is still standard in other characters, such as 澄 (1.1704).

2973 back [old] 裡
R-2602

cloak . . . computer. [12]

The transposition of the standard form 裏 (1.399) involves moving the computer from the middle of the element for cloak to the right.

2974 park [alternate] 薗
R-3188

flowers . . . park. [16]

This character is used principally in proper names. The only change you will notice from the standard form 園 (1.585) is the addition of the element for *flowers*.

2975 shop [alternate] 鋪
R-2683

metal . . . dog tag. [15]

The only difference from the more common form 舗 (1.1839) is that the left side here uses the element for *metal*. There is also a third alternative which is sometimes seen, but has been omitted here: 舖.

2976   island [alternate]
R-3187

嶋

mountain . . . bird. [14]

The alternate form is used mainly in names. It differs from the standard form 鳥 only in the positioning of the *mountain*.

2977   summit [alternate]
R-3196

峯

mountain . . . walking legs . . . bushes. [10]

The alternate form is used mainly in names. As in the character in the previous frame, the only difference from the standard form 峰 (1.1562) is in the positioning of the *mountain*.

2978   boulder [old]
R-3193

巖

mountain . . . stern. [20]

The simplified character was learned as 岩 (1.770).

2979   plains [old]
R-3200

埜

grove . . . soil. [11]

The standard form 野 (1.1596) differs rather radically from this older form, which appears now in old texts and occasionally in proper names.

2980   Bldg. [old]
R-3197

舘

umbrella . . . tongue . . . bureaucrat. [16]

The standard form of this character 館 (1.1478) uses the element for *food* on the left. Because the older form is somewhat simpler to write, it remains in use today.

2981   dragon [old]
R-3189

龍

vase . . . meat . . . slingshot (doubled up with a) *snake . . . three . . . clothes.* [16]

The older form 龍 (1.536) was actually learned in VOL. 1 in connection with the character for **attack** 襲 (1.2025), and will appear in the following frame as well. This older form is still used widely today. In addition to the new characters in the following two frames, note the following example also already learned:

OLD FORM	MODERN ABBREVIATION
瀧	滝 (1.537)

2982	patronage	寵

R-2922

house . . . dragon [old]. [19]

2983	deafness	聾

R-2869

dragon [old] *. . . ear.* [22]

2984	longing [old]	慾

R-3198

longing . . . heart. [15]

The only difference from the standard form of this character 欲 (1.92) is that the element for *heart* is included at the bottom.

2985	span [old]	瓦

R-3201

tile . . . floor. [6]

The standard form of this character 亙 (1.32) is also standard when it is used as a primitive in other characters. Note the following example in a character already learned:

OLD FORM	MODERN ABBREVIATION
恆	恒 (1.620)

2986	body [old]	躯

R-2712

somebody . . . ward. [11]

The standard form 身 (1.1248) has by and large replaced this older character today.

2987 Point [old]
R-3192

mountain ... prison. [17]

The abbreviated form of this character 岳 (1.1330), used in place names, shifts the *mountain* to the bottom, a rather odd change as the kanji go.

2988 country [old]
R-3186

pent-up ... a. [11]

The element that replaces *jewel* in the standard form of this character 国 (1.581) is among the new kanji learned in this book (see FRAME 2091 above).

We end this chapter with those characters in fairly common use whose elements have *not* been assigned newer abbreviations.

2989 shin
R-2525

flesh ... ceiling ... flood ... craft. [11]

The element on the right, which will appear once more in the following frame, is actually the old form of the element for *spool,* 坙, and replaces it in the old form of all the kanji we learned with that element. In addition to the following frame, here are two more examples:

OLD FORM	MODERN ABBREVIATION
輕	軽 (1.717)
經	経 (1.1360)

2990 formidable
R-2524

ceiling ... flood ... craft ... muscle. [9]

2991 stationary
R-2659

bamboo ... float. [12]

The standard abbreviation one would have expected here—and which is likely to appear in official lists in the years ahead—appears in the following examples of common newer forms you already know:

OLD FORM	MODERN ABBREVIATION
踐	践 (1.1286)
棧	桟 (1.367)
錢	銭 (1.368)
賤	賎 (2.2735)

2992   enshrine   祀
R-3031

altar . . . snake. [8]

The standard abbreviation for *altar* has generally taken over, but the character in this and the following frame are exceptions.

2993   exorcism   祓
R-3032

altar . . . chihuahua with an extra leg. [10]

Think of the "five-legged" *dog* here as some kind of an evil spirit that has to be driven out, and the odd shape should be easy to remember.

2994   dither   躇
R-2737

wooden leg . . . renowned. [19]

The old form here is the element *puppet* which forms part of the primitive for *renowned* here. The difference is the addition of a final *drop*. This has generally disappeared today, as in the following examples:

OLD FORM	MODERN ABBREVIATION
堵	堵 (1.2192)
渚	渚 (1.1263)
曙	曙 (2.2448)
箸	箸 (2.2640)

2995 longevity [old] 壽
R-3185

lidded crock ... broken crown ... craft ... floor ... mouth ... glue. [14]

The newer form 寿 (1.1565) tends to dominate today when it is used as a primitive. Note the following example:

OLD FORM	MODERN ABBREVIATION
鑄	鋳 (1.717)

2996 hesitate 躊
R-3053

wooden leg ... longevity. [14]

2997 glossary 彙
R-3084

The primitive of this character is actually an old form of *broom* ⺕. The remaining elements are: *crown ... fruit.* [13]

2998 bean jam 饅
R-2345

food ... mandala. [20]

It is only a matter of time before this character takes the standard abbreviation for *food* on the left. Meantime, it will alert you to the older style of writing, which still shows up in rather complicated characters that use the *food* primitive.

2999 retch 嘔
R-3184

mouth ... ward. [14]

The standard abbreviation of the element to the right can be seen from the following examples:

OLD FORM	MODERN ABBREVIATION
區	区 (1.1696)
歐	欧 (1.1698)
毆	殴 (1.1699)

3000　snapping turtle 鼈

R-3088

shredder . . . eels [old form]. [25]

The change in the first three strokes of the element for *shredder* is a familiar one found often in older forms. I leave it to you to combine the pieces for the old form of *eels*. Learning stroke order will help considerably:

The older form of the primitive we learned as *eels* is rather more difficult. You will find it in older forms of several familiar characters such as the following:

OLD FORM	MODERN ABBREVIATION
繩	縄 (1.1377)
蠅	蝿 (2.2685)

PART TWO

Reading

CHAPTER 7

Old Pure Groups

THE FIRST GROUP of readings center on what were called in *Remembering the Kanji 2* "Pure Groups." Each character that belongs to a pure group contains a **signal primitive** which prescribes a given *on-yomi* for that character and all others in the group with it.

The number to the far right of the top line set in bold type indicates the frame number in which the writing of the kanji was introduced. In almost all cases this refers to a frame in Part One of the present volume.

The number under the character in each frame is preceded by an "R-" to indicate that it refers to a reading frame. These numbers begin where VOL. 2 left off.

Unlike VOL. 2, the frames also include not only *on-yomi* but *kun-yomi* as well. In some cases, the "assigned" readings are almost never used, or used only for names. Because the number of special readings for names is virtually limitless, only the 274 characters approved by the Ministry of Education are supplied with *on-yomi* for use in names.

For further information about the layout of the frames, see page 8.

We begin this chapter with groups whose signal primitives were already introduced in VOL. 2. The signal primitive, its pronunciation, and characters belonging to the same appear in a separate frame at the head of each section.

The number under the characters in the group frames refers to the frame in VOL. 2. which introduced the reading (hence the "R-" preceding it.) Where a number is missing, the single primitive in question was learned only as a primitive element, not as a kanji.

白	ハク	泊	迫	拍	舶	伯
R-89		R-90	R-91	R-92	R-93	R-94

狛		ハク			2343
R-2244	狛	こま		lion-dog	

箔		ハク			2634
R-2245	金箔	キンパク	gold leaf		

粕		ハク			2648
R-2246	糟粕	ソウハク	lees; dregs		
	粕	かす	lees		

青	セイ	精	清	晴	静	請	情
R-78		R-79	R-80	R-81	R-82	R-83	R-84

靖		セイ			2621
R-2247	靖国	セイコク	a country ruled in peace		
	靖	のぶ	used in names		
	靖	やす	used in names		
	靖	やすし	used in names		

錆		セイ			2771
R-2248	防錆	ボウセイ	protection against rust		
	錆	さび	rust		

包	ホウ	砲	泡	抱	胞	飽
R-95		R-96	R-97	R-98	R-99	R-100

庖		ホウ			2234
R-2249	庖丁	ホウチョウ	kitchen knife		

可	カ	何	荷	歌	河
R-105		R-106	R-107	R-108	R-109

苛		カ			2373
R-2250	苛酷	カコク	harshness; severity		
	苛める	いじめる	to bully		
	苛つ	いらだつ	be irritated		

僉	ケン	俭	験	険	検	剣
		R-131	R-132	R-133	R-134	R-135

鹸	ケン			2867
R-2251	石鹸	セッケン	soap	

商	テキ	適	敵	嫡	摘	滴
		R-157	R-158	R-159	R-160	R-161

鏑	テキ		2758
R-2252	鳴鏑	メイテキ	whistle of an arrow
	鏑	かぶら	arrowhead

且	ソ	組	祖	租	粗	阻
R-661		R-148	R-149	R-150	R-151	R-152

狙	ソ		2344
R-2253	狙撃兵	ソゲキヘイ	sniper; marksman
	狙う	ねらう	take aim

司	シ	詞	飼	伺	嗣
R-122		R-123	R-124	R-125	R-126

笥	シ・ス		2635
R-2254	笥金	シキン	gold put in box
	箪笥	タンス	cabinet

付	フ	府	符	附	腐
R-69		R-70	R-71	R-72	R-73

腑	フ		2456
R-2255	腑に落ちる	ふにおちる	to catch on; "click"

官	カン	管	棺	館
R-127		R-128	R-129	R-130

菅		カン		2410
R-2256	菅家	カンケ	Sugawara family	

Note how the family is referred to by using the *on-yomi* of the first character of their full name. Note also the unusual *kun-yomi* in the name *Suga*wara. The standard reading is:

菅	すげ	sedge

義	ギ	議	儀	犠
R-74		R-75	R-76	R-77

蟻		ギ		2686
R-2257	蟻酸	ギサン	formic acid	
	蟻	あり	ant	

襄	ジョウ	嬢	譲	壌	醸
		R-101	R-102	R-103	R-104

穣		ジョウ・ニョウ		2609
R-2258	穣歳	ジョウサイ	bumper crop	
	穣る	みのる	bear fruit; fructify	
	穣か	ゆたか	fruitful	
	穣	おさむ	used in names	
	穣	みのる	used in names	
	穣	ゆたか	used in names	

半	ハン	判	畔	伴
R-166		R-167	R-168	R-169

絆		ハン・バン		2658
R-2259	脚絆	キャハン	leggings; gaiters	
	絆創膏	バンソウコウ	adhesive plaster (for wounds)	
	絆	きずな	bands; ties; shackles	

		絆ぐ	つなぐ	be attached

曹 ソウ	槽	遭	漕	
R-174	R-175	R-176	R-177	

糟		ソウ		2649
R-2260	糟粕	ソウハク	dregs	

俞 ユ	輸	愉	諭	癒
	R-178	R-179	R-180	R-181

愈		ユ		2433
R-2261	愈々	ユユ	more and more severe	
	愈	いよいよ	increasingly	

尞 リョウ	僚	寮	療	
	R-239	R-240	R-241	

瞭		リョウ		2582
R-2262	明瞭	メイリョウ	clear; patent	
	瞭らか	あきらか	evident; obvious	
	瞭	あき	used in names	
	瞭	あきら	used in names	

遼		リョウ		2419
R-2263	遼遠	リョウエン	distant; remote	
	遼か	はるか	far off in the distance	

燎		リョウ		2535
R-2264	燎原の火	リョウゲンのひ	wildfire; prairie fire	
	燎	かかりび	watchfire	
	燎く	やく	to burn	

夾	キョウ	峽	狹	挟
		R-290	R-291	R-292

俠		キョウ		2107
R-2265	義俠	ギキョウ	chivalry	

頰		キョウ		2792
R-2266	頰舌	キョウゼツ	eloquence	
	頰	ほお	cheek	

昌	ショウ	唱	晶	
R-580		R-308	R-309	

菖		ショウ		2366
R-2267	菖蒲	ショウブ	iris	
	菖	あやめ	used in names	

娼		ショウ		2198
R-2268	娼婦	ショウフ	harlot	

扁	ヘン	編	偏	遍
		R-203	R-204	R-205

騙		ヘン		2806
R-2269	騙欺	ヘンキ	deception	
	騙る	かたる	swindle; cheat; misrepresent	
	騙す	だます	to deceive; trick	

篇		ヘン		2645
R-2270	前篇	ゼンペン	Part One	

及	キュウ	吸	級
R-185		R-186	R-187

汲		キュウ		2322
R-2271	汲水	キュウスイ	drawing water	
	汲む	くむ	draw water	

笈		キュウ		2644
R-2272	笈	おい	creel	

亢	コウ	坑	航	抗
		R-221	R-222	R-223

杭		コウ		2484
R-2273	杭州	コウシュウ	ancient Chinese capital	
	杭	くい	picket	

票	ヒョウ	漂	標
R-206		R-207	R-208

瓢		ヒョウ		2911
R-2274	瓢箪	ヒョウタン	bottle gourd	
	瓢	ひさご	gourd; calabash	
	瓢	ふくべ	gourd; calabash	

苗	ビョウ	描	猫
R-278		R-279	R-280

錨		ビョウ		2765
R-2275	錨鎖	ビョウサ	chain cable; hawser	
	錨	いかり	anchor; killick	

廷	テイ	艇	庭		
R-212		R-213	R-214		

挺		テイ・チョウ			2267
R-2276	挺身隊	テイシンタイ	volunteer corps		
	挺く	ぬく	pull out		

朋	ホウ	崩			
R-354		R-355			

鵬		ホウ			2829
R-2277	鵬	おおとり	phoenix; large mythical bird		
	鵬	とも	used in names		
	鵬	ゆき	used in names		

代	タイ	貸	袋		
R-269		R-270	R-271		

黛		タイ			2864
R-2278	黛青	タイセイ	blackish blue		
	黛	まゆずみ	used in names		

末	マツ	沫	抹		
R-284		R-285	R-286		

茉		マツ・マ			2348
R-2279	茉莉花	マツリカ	jasmine		

利	リ	梨	痢		
R-236		R-237	R-238		

莉		リ			2349
R-2280	茉莉花	マツリカ	jasmine		

屈	クツ	掘	
R-302		R-303	

窟		クツ	2615
R-2281	岩窟	ガンクツ	cave; rocky cavern

夆	ホウ	縫	峰
		R-352	R-353

逢		ホウ	2417
R-2282	逢着	ホウチャク	face; encounter
	逢える	むかえる	go to meet
	逢う	あう	to encounter

蓬		ホウ	2375
R-2283	蓬莱	ホウライ	legendary Chinese Isle of Eternal Youth
	蓬	よもぎ	mugwort

蜂		ホウ	2687
R-2284	蜂房	ホウボウ	honeycomb; beehive
	蜂	はち	bee

鋒		ホウ	2768
R-2285	論鋒	ロンポウ	line of argument

我	ガ	餓	
R-338		R-339	

俄		ガ	2110
R-2286	俄然	ガゼン	suddenly; abruptly
	俄か	にわか	sudden

峨		ガ		2226
R-2287	嵯峨	サガ	town near Kyoto	

蛾		ガ		2694
R-2288	蛾	ガ	moth	

安	アン	案	
R-314		R-315	

按		アン		2259
R-2289	按摩	アンマ	massage; masseur	

鞍		アン		2782
R-2290	鞍馬	アンバ	pommel; sidehorse	
	鞍	くら	saddle	

晏		アン		2442
R-2291	晏如	アンジョ	at ease; comfort	
	晏い	おそい	tardy; slow	
	晏らか	やすらか	at ease	
	晏	さだ	used in names	
	晏	はる	used in names	
	晏	やす	used in names	

玄	ゲン	弦	
R-528		R-529	

絃		ゲン		2669
R-2292	管絃楽団	カンゲンガクダン	orchestra	
	絃	いと	string (on a violin, etc.)	
	絃	つる	used in names	

舷		ゲン		2675
R-2293	舷窓	ゲンソウ	porthole	

眩		ゲン		2581
R-2294	眩惑	ゲンワク	bewilderment	
	眩めく	くるめく	feel dizzy	
	眩しい	まぶしい	dizzy; dazzled	

倉	ソウ	創	
R-472		R-473	

槍		ソウ		2516
R-2295	槍術	ソウジュツ	spearsmanship	
	槍	やり	spear; lance	

蒼		ソウ		2399
R-2296	蒼白	ソウハク	pale; ashen	
	蒼い	あおい	pale blue	
	蒼	しげる	used in names	

路	ロ	露	
R-448		R-449	

鷺		ロ		2833
R-2297	鷺羽	ロウ	heron wings	
	鷺	さぎ	heron	

蕗		ロ		2370
R-2298	蕗	ふき	bog rhubarb; coltsfoot	

容	ヨウ	溶
R-478		R-479

熔		ヨウ		2547
R-2299	熔接	ヨウセツ	welding	
	熔かす	とかす	melt (metals)	
	熔ける	とける	be melted (metals)	

蓉		ヨウ		2362
R-2300	芙蓉	フヨウ	lotus; cotton rose	

元	ガン	頑
R-298		R-299

玩		ガン		2567
R-2301	玩具	ガング	toys	
	玩ぶ	もてあそぶ	toy with	

翫		ガン		2899
R-2302	翫味	ガンミ	savor; appreciate	
	翫ぶ	もてあそぶ	toy with	

幾	キ	機
R-300		R-301

磯		キ		2594
R-2303	磯	いそ	rocky beach	

畿		キ		2887
R-2304	近畿	キンキ	region around Kyoto–Osaka	

需 ジュ 儒			
R-366　　　R-367			

嬬		ジュ	2203
R-2305	嬬	つま	wife

濡		ジュ	2329
R-2306	濡首	じゅしゅ	dead drunk
	濡れる	ぬれる	become wet; be impassioned

秋 シュウ 愁			
R-482　　　R-483			

鍬		シュウ	2762
R-2307	鍬	くわ	hoe

萩		シュウ	2351
R-2308	萩	はぎ	Japanese bush clover

焦 ショウ 礁			
R-512　　　R-513			

樵		ショウ	2478
R-2309	樵夫	ショウフ	woodcutter; lumberjack
	樵	きこり	woodcutter
	樵る	こる	cut wood

蕉		ショウ	2367
R-2310	芭蕉	バショウ	Bashō (haiku poet)

帝	テイ	締
R-462		R-463

諦		テイ・タイ		2716
R-2311	諦観	テイカン	clear vision	
	四諦	シタイ	Four Noble Truths of Buddhism	
	諦める	あきらめる	give up; abandon	

蹄		テイ		2741
R-2312	蹄形	テイケイ	U-shaped	
	蹄	ひづめ	hoof	

菫	キン	勤	謹
		R-412	R-413

僅		キン		2116
R-2313	僅少	キンショウ	few; little; meagre	
	僅かに	わずかに	a few	

菫		キン・コン		2099
R-2314	菫菜	キンサイ	Dutch trefoil; wild celery	
	菫	すみれ	violet	

䍃	ヨウ	謡	揺
		R-474	R-475

遥		ヨウ		2418
R-2315	遥拝	ヨウハイ	worship from a distance	
	遥かに	はるかに	far off; in the distance	

瑶		ヨウ		2553
R-2316	瑶顔	ヨウガン	beautiful face	
	瑶	たま	beautiful stone	

童 ドウ			
R-1571			

憧		ドウ・ショウ	2280
R-2317	憧憬	ドウケイ	yearning; hankering
	憧れる	あこがれる	aspire for; be drawn to

撞		ドウ・トウ・シュ	2245
R-2318	撞球	ドウキュウ	billiards
	撞木	シュモク	log used to strike a bell
	撞く	つく	strike against

求 キュウ	救	球	
R-230	R-231	R-232	

毬		キュウ	2533
R-2319	毬子	キュウシ	ball; type of chrysanthemum
	毬	まり	ball

敝 ヘイ	幣	弊	
	R-344	R-345	

蔽		ヘイ	2358
R-2320	遮蔽	シャヘイ	cover; shelter
	蔽う	おおう	to cover; to conceal
	蔽い	くらい	dark; hidden

瞥		ベツ	2927
R-2321	瞥見	ベッケン	glance; a peek at

州	シュウ	酬	
R-257		R-259	

洲		シュウ		2289
R-2322	五大洲	ゴダイシュウ	the five continents	
	洲	す	sandbar; sandbank	
	洲	しま	island	
	洲	くに	used in names	

然	ネン	燃	
R-440		R-441	

撚		ネン		2266
R-2323	撚糸	ネンシ	silk throwing	
	撚る	ひねる	twist; tweak	
	撚	より	a twist; ply	

将	ショウ	奨	
R-514		R-515	

醤		ショウ		2746
R-2324	醤油	ショウユ	soy sauce	

貞	テイ	偵	
R-312		R-313	

禎		テイ		2603
R-2325	禎祥	テイショウ	propitious	
	禎しい	ただしい	upright	
	禎い	さいわい	happy	
	禎	ただ	used in names	
	禎	さち	used in names	
	禎	つぐ	used in names	
	禎	よし	used for names	

受	ジュ	授	
R-364		R-365	

綬		ジュ	2672
R-2326	印綬	インジュ	ribbon (of an official seal)
	綬	ひも	cord
	綬	くみひも	braided cord

建	ケン	健	
R-406		R-407	

鍵		ケン	2761
R-2327	鍵盤	ケンバン	keyboard; clavier
	鍵	かぎ	key

侯	コウ	候	
R-416		R-417	

喉		コウ	2164
R-2328	喉頭炎	コウトウエン	laryngitis
	喉	のど	throat

伐	バツ	閥	
R-316		R-317	

筏		バツ	2629
R-2329	筏	いかだ	raft

足	ソク	促	
R-336		R-337	

捉		ソク	2260
R-2330	捕捉	ホソク	capture; apprehension
	捉える	とらえる	catch; grab hold of

農	ノウ	濃
R-444		R-445

膿		ノウ		2455
R-2331	化膿	カノウ	pyosis; turning to pus	
	膿む	うむ	to fester	

郷	キョウ	響
R-430		R-431

饗		キョウ		2799
R-2332	饗宴	キョウエン	banquet	

会	カイ	絵
R-382		R-383

桧		カイ		2495
R-2333	桧	ひのき	Japanese cypress	

介	カイ	界
R-380		R-381

芥		カイ・ケ		2376
R-2334	塵芥	ジンカイ	rubbish	
	芥子粒	ケシつぶ	poppy seed	
	芥子	からし	mustard	
	芥	あくた	dirt; trash	

善	ゼン	繕		
R-486		R-487		

膳		ゼン		2468
R-2335	膳	ゼン	small dining table on tray	

泉	セン	線		
R-502		R-503		

腺		セン		2466
R-2336	前立腺	ゼンリツセン	prostate	

乇	タク	宅	託	
		R-458	R-459	

托		タク		2264
R-2337	托鉢	タクハツ	religious mendicancy	

暴	バク	爆		
R-318		R-319		

曝		バク		2447
R-2338	曝露	バクロ	exposure	

悤	ソウ	総	窓	
		R-306	R-307	

聡		ソウ		2677
R-2339	聡明	ソウメイ	wisdom; sagacity	
	聡	あき	used in names	
	聡	あきら	used in names	
	聡	さと	used in names	
	聡	さとし	used in names	

| | 聡 | とし | used in names |
| | 聡 | とき | used in names |

| 录 | ロク | 録 | 緑 |
| | | R-296 | R-297 |

禄		ロク		2602
R-2340	俸禄	ホウロク	stipend; salary
	禄	ち	used in names
	禄	とし	used in names
	禄	とみ	used in names
	禄	よし	used in names

| 呈 | テイ | 程 |
| R-460 | | R-461 |

逞		テイ		2971
R-2341	不逞	フテイ	insubordination
	逞しい	たくましい	stalwart

| 充 | リュウ | 流 | 硫 |
| | | R-496 | R-497 |

| 琉 | | リュウ | | 2557 |
| R-2342 | 琉球 | リュウキュウ | the Loochoo islands |

| 密 | ミツ | 蜜 |
| R-534 | | R-535 |

| 樒 | | ミツ | | 2532 |
| R-2343 | 樒 | しきみ | Japanese star anise |

工	コウ	功	攻	江	紅	項	貢	巧
R-114		R-115	R-116	R-117	R-118	R-119	R-120	R-121

肛		コウ		2459
R-2344	肛門	コウモン	anus	

NB: When this group was introduced in VOL. 2, it was noted that the primitive element must occupy a *prominent place* in order to serve as a signal primitive.

We conclude this chapter with three pure groups using kanji that appeared in VOL. 2 only as primitives. This is indicated by a downward arrow (↓) in place of the frame number.

曼	マン	慢	漫
↓		R-434	R-435

饅		マン		2998
R-2345	饅頭	マンジュウ	steamed bun (Chinese)	

鰻		マン		2811
R-2346	鰻	うなぎ	eel	

曼		マン		2100
R-2347	曼陀羅	マンダラ	mandala	

蔓		マン		2359
R-2348	蔓延	マンエン	spreading; diffusion	
	蔓	つる	vine; tendril	

喬	キョウ	橋	矯	嬌
↓		R-293	R-294	R-295

僑		キョウ		2120
R-2349	華僑	カキョウ	overseas Chinese	

喬		キョウ		2104
R-2350	喬木	キョウボク	tall tree	
	喬い	たかい	tall	
	喬	たか	used in names	
	喬	たかし	used in names	

蕎		キョウ		2369
R-2351	蕎麦	そば	buckwheat noodles	

CHAPTER 8

New Pure Groups

THIS CHAPTER introduces new primitive groups, based on signal primitives that were not introduced as such in VOL. 2. As before, a small frame will be set at the head of each group to indicate the signal primitive, reading, and kanji from VOL. 2 that belong to this group.

In most cases, the reading of the kanji that will serve here as a signal primitive has already been learned, and in that case the reference to the frame in VOL. 2 where the reading was introduced will appear under the signal primitive.

As in the previous chapter, an arrow (↓) below a signal primitive will indicate that it is in fact a kanji introduced in this volume. Where there is no arrow or frame number, the signal primitive has not been learned as a kanji. For further information on the layout of the frames, see page 8.

We may begin with groups based on kanji whose principal *on-yomi* has already been learned. Since the majority of the signal primitives have already been included in VOL. 2, most of these groups will be small, often with only one new reading to learn.

夌	リョウ	陵
	R-1946	

稜		リョウ・ロウ		2610
R-2352	山稜	サンリョウ	mountain ridge	
	稜	かど	corner	
	稜	いず	used in names	
	稜	たか	used in names	
凌		リョウ		2136
R-2353	凌駕	リョウガ	excel; surpass	
	凌ぐ	しのぐ	endure; bear	

峻		リョウ		2225
R-2354	峻層	リョウソウ	high and overtowering	

綾		リョウ・リン		2668
R-2355	綾南町	リョウナンチョウ	city in Kagawa Prefecture	
	綾	あや	used in names	

坐	ザ	座	
↓		R-574	

坐		ザ		2844
R-2356	坐禅	ザゼン	Zen meditation	
	坐る	すわる	sit	

挫		ザ		2845
R-2357	捻挫	ネンザ	sprain	

巽	セン	選	
↓		R-1052	

撰		セン		2253
R-2358	撰集	センシュウ	anthology	
	撰ぶ	えらぶ	pick out; select	

巽		ソン		2861
R-2359	巽位	ソンイ	southeast direction	
	巽	たつみ	southeast (dragon-snake)	
	巽	ゆく	used in names	
	巽	よし	used in names	

菊 キク 菊			
R-555			

鞠 R-2360		キク	2787
	鞠問	キクモン	interrogation of a criminal
	鞠	まり	ball; used in names
	鞠ぐ	つぐ	to follow; used in names
	鞠	みつ	used in names

麴 R-2361		キク	2753
	麴室	キクシツ	shed for storing rice malt
	麴	こうじ	malted rice

就 シュウ			
R-1689			

蹴 R-2362		シュウ	2742
	蹴球	シュウキュウ	football
	蹴る	ける	to kick

鷲 R-2363		シュウ	2834
	鷲	わし	eagle

差 サ			
R-1815			

嵯 R-2364		サ	2230
	嵯峨	サガ	town near Kyoto

瑳 R-2365		サ	2559
	瑳々	ササ	shining white (of stones)
	瑳く	みがく	to polish (stones)

夸	コ	誇
R-1977		

跨		コ・カ		2744
R-2366	跨線橋	コセンキョウ	overpass	
	跨ぐ	またぐ	straddle	

袴		コ		2626
R-2367	袴	はかま	hakama skirt	

厉	レイ	励
R-2067		

蛎		レイ		2697
R-2368	蛎	かき	oyster	

砺		レイ		2595
R-2369	砺	と	grindstone	
	砺く	みがく	to polish	
	砺ぐ	とぐ	whet; sharpen	

鹿	ロク	
R-2229		

漉		ロク		2304
R-2370	漉酒	ロクシュ	filtering saké	
	漉	こし	a filter	
	漉す	こす	to strain; filter	
	漉く	すく	make paper	

麓		ロク		2839
R-2371	山麓	サンロク	foot of a mountain	
	麓	ふもと	foothills	

華 カ				
R-1151				

樺		カ		2515
R-2372	樺燭	カショク	birchbark-type torch	
	樺	か(ん)ば	birch	

嘩		カ		2160
R-2373	喧嘩	ケンカ	quarrel	

叚 カ 暇				
R-1817				

蝦		カ		2689
R-2374	蝦	えび	shrimp	

霞		カ		2779
R-2375	煙霞	エンカ	smoke and mist; scenic views	
	霞む	かすむ	be hazy; grow dim	
	霞	かすみ	haze; mist	

規 キ				
R-826				

窺		キ		2613
R-2376	窺知	キチ	perceive; grasp	
	窺う	うかがう	peep; spy on	
	窺	うかがい	a guess; an inquiry	

槻		キ		2527
R-2377	槻	けやき	zelkova tree	
	槻	つき	zelkova tree	

豪 ゴウ			
R-1883			

濠		ゴウ		2306
R-2378	濠州	ゴウシュウ	Australia	
	濠	ほり	moat	

壕		ゴウ		2186
R-2379	防空壕	ボウクウゴウ	air-raid shelter	
	壕	ほり	ditch; trench	

蚤 ソウ 騒			
R-1993			

搔		ソウ		2252
R-2380	搔痒	ソウヨウ	itching	
	搔く	かく	to scratch	

蚤		ソウ		2681
R-2381	蚤起	ソウキ	rise early	
	蚤	のみ	flea	

叟 ソウ 捜			
R-1670			

痩		ソウ		2577
R-2382	痩身	ソウシン	slender body; thin build	
	痩ける	こける	be sunken; be hollow	
	痩せる	やせる	lose weight	

艘		ソウ		2068
R-2383	一艘	イッソウ	one ship	
	艘	ふね	ship	

久	キュウ		
R-1638			

玖		キュウ		2565
R-2384	玖	たま	jewel; used in names	
	玖	ひさ	used in names	

灸		キュウ		2538
R-2385	灸	キュウ	moxa cautery	

追	ツイ		
R-1642			

槌		ツイ		2477
R-2386	鉄槌	テッツイ	iron hammer	
	槌	つち	hammer	

鎚		ツイ		2769
R-2387	鉄鎚	テッツイ	iron hammer	

居	キョ		
R-1220			

鋸		キョ		2759
R-2388	鋸歯状	キョシジョウ	indentation; saw-toothed	
	鋸	のこぎり	a saw	

裾		キョ		2624
R-2389	裾	すそ	hem	

| 妻 サイ・セイ R-1903 | | | | |

凄 R-2390		セイ		2133
	凄艶	セイエン	weirdly beautiful	
	凄い	すごい	tremendous; awesome	

棲 R-2391		セイ		2496
	同棲	ドウセイ	co-habitation	
	棲む	すむ	live; dwell	

| 孟 モウ 猛 ↓ R-1730 | | | | |

孟 R-2392		モウ		2872
	孟子	モウシ	Mencius	
	孟	たけし	used in names	
	孟	はじめ	used in names	

| 于 ゥ 宇 R-30 | | | | |

迂 R-2393		ゥ		2415
	迂回	ウカイ	detour	

| 丞 ジョウ 蒸 ↓ R-1964 | | | | |

丞 R-2394		ジョウ・ショウ		2919
	丞相	ジョウショウ	Chancellor	
	丞む	すすむ	go forwards; advance	
	丞	すけ	used in names	
	丞	たすく	used in names	

面 メン				
R-1098				

麺		メン		2752
R-2395	麺類	メンルイ	noodles	

帛 メン 綿				
		R-1871		

棉		メン		2512
R-2396	棉花	メンカ	raw cotton	
	棉	わた	cotton	

玨 ハン 班				
		R-1750		

斑		ハン		2556
R-2397	蒙古斑	モウコハン	infant's "Mongolian spot"	
	斑	まだら	spots; patches; streaks	

完 カン				
R-989				

莞		カン		2408
R-2398	莞爾	カンジ	with a smile	
	莞	いぐさ	kind of rush; used in names	

孫 ソン				
R-874				

遜		ソン		2422
R-2399	謙遜	ケンソン	humility	
	遜る	へりくだる	to be humble	

闌	ラン	欄
R-1935		

蘭		ラン		2363
R-2400	蘭学	ランガク	studying Western science in the Dutch language	

御	ギョ
R-1950	

禦		ギョ		2597
R-2401	防禦	ボウギョ	defense	
	禦ぐ	ふせぐ	ward off	

扇	セン
R-1660	

煽		セン		2540
R-2402	煽動	センドウ	agitation; demagoguery	
	煽る	あおる	fan the flames	
	煽てる	おだてる	incite; instigate	

喜	キ
R-1859	

嬉		キ		2207
R-2403	嬉戯	キギ	frolicking	
	嬉しい	うれしい	happy	
	嬉しむ	たのしむ	rejoice; enjoy	
	嬉	よし	used in names	

陰 イン			
R-1931			

蔭		イン	2374
R-2404	緑蔭	リョクイン	shady nook
	蔭	かげ	shade; shadow

勇 ユウ			
R-1790			

湧		ユウ・ヨウ	2284
R-2405	湧出	ユウシュツ	gushing out
	湧く	わく	gush up

庸 ヨウ			
R-2219			

傭		ヨウ	2128
R-2406	傭兵	ヨウヘイ	mercenary soldier
	傭う	やとう	to employ

殿 デン			
R-2046			

澱		デン	2300
R-2407	澱粉	デンプン	starch
	澱	おり	dregs; sediment
	澱む	よどむ	stagnate

丈 ジョウ			
R-961			

杖		ジョウ	2504
R-2408	杖罪	ジョウザイ	flogging; caning
	杖	つえ	cane; walking stick

后	コウ
R-1857	

垢		コウ・ク		2187
R-2409	垢塵	コウジン	dirt; filth	
	無垢	ムク	immaculate; undefiled	
	垢	あか	stain	

筑	チク	築
↓		R-1617

筑		チク		2637
R-2410	筑前	チクゼン	old name for northwest part of Fukuoka prefecture	

斬	ザン	暫
↓		R-2010

斬		ザン		2092
R-2411	斬首	ザンシュ	decapitation	
	斬る	きる	cut down; behead	

赫	カク	嚇
↓		R-2215

赫		カク		2908
R-2412	赫々	カッカク	splendid; distinguished	

奥	オウ
R-2132	

襖		オウ		2627
R-2413	襖	ふすま	sliding door or screen	

胃 イ
R-1809

謂		イ		2725
R-2414	謂う	いう	to say	
	謂われ	いわれ	reason; grounds	

亜 ア
R-1818

唖		ア		2958
R-2415	唖然	アゼン	flabbergasted	

解 カイ
R-1572

蟹		カイ		2682
R-2416	蟹行	カイコウ	walking sideways	
	蟹	かに	crab	

覚 カク
R-1849

撹		カク・コウ		2257
R-2417	撹乱	カクラン	disturbance; turbulence	

宜 ギ
R-1828

誼		ギ		2719
R-2418	交誼	コウギ	friendship; amity	
	誼み	よしみ	goodwill; friendly relations	
	誼	よし	used in names	

困	コン
R-1673	

梱		コン		2518
R-2419	梱包	コンポウ	packing; crating	
	梱	こり	a bale; package	

算	サン
R-1669	

纂		サン		2641
R-2420	編纂	ヘンサン	compilation; editing	

賛	サン
R-1740	

讃		サン		2711
R-2421	讃美歌	サンビカ	hymn; song of praise	
	讃える	たたえる	give praise to	

頃	ケイ	傾
↓		R-1756

頃		ケイ		2791
R-2422	頃	ころ	around; about	
	頃	ごろ	time; about	

思	シ
R-1568	

偲		シ		2129
R-2423	偲ぶ	しのぶ	recall; reminisce	

師	シ
R-1819	

獅		シ		2345
R-2424	獅子	シシ	lion	

亶	タン	壇
		R-718

檀		ダン・タン		2525
R-2425	檀家	ダンカ	parishoner of a temple	
	黒檀	コクタン	ebony	
	檀	まゆみ	spindle tree	

隼	ジュン	準
↓		R-1767

隼		ジュン・シュン		2879
R-2426	隼	はやぶさ	peregrine falcon	
	隼	はや	used in names	

如	ジョ
R-1845	

恕		ジョ		2434
R-2427	宥恕	ユウジョ	pardon; forgiveness	
	恕す	ゆるす	sanction; pardon	
	恕	ただし	used in names	
	恕	のり	used in names	
	恕	ひろし	used in names	
	恕	ゆき	used in names	
	恕	しのぶ	used in names	

助	ジョ
R-1558	

鋤		ジョ		2756
R-2428	鋤簾	ジョレン	small hand scoop	
	鋤	すき	a plow; spade	

疾	シツ
R-1923	

嫉		シツ		2202
R-2429	嫉妬	シット	jealousy; envy	
	嫉む	そねむ	be jealous	
	嫉む	ねたむ	to envy	

桼	シツ	漆
		R-1907

膝		シツ		2461
R-2430	膝下	シッカ	at one's knees or feet	
	膝	ひざ	knee; lap	

香	キョウ
R-2095	

馨		キョウ・ケイ		2925
R-2431	馨	かおり	a fragrance; used in names	
	馨る	かおる	smell fragrant	
	馨	か	used in names	
	馨	かおる	used in names	
	馨	きよ	used in names	

晏	エン	宴
		R-1723

堰		エン		2191
R-2432	堰堤	エンテイ	dam; weir	
	堰	せき	dam; sluice	

太	タ	駄
R-19		R-1780

汰		タ・タイ		2316
R-2433	無沙汰	ブサタ	neglect to call on or write to	

英	エイ
R-827	

瑛		エイ		2566
R-2434	瑛子	エイこ	Eiko (woman's name)	

頻	ヒン
R-1944	

瀕		ヒン		2305
R-2435	瀕死状態	ヒンシジョウタイ	in a state near death	

愛	アイ
R-1096	

曖		アイ		2437
R-2436	曖昧	アイマイ	vague; ambiguous	

康 コウ
R-1149

糠		コウ		2652
R-2437	糟糠	ソウコウ	chaff and bran; poverty	
	糠	ぬか	rice bran	

卂 ジン 迅
R-1569

訊		ジン		2713
R-2438	訊問	ジンモン	interrogation	
	訊ねる	たずねる	to question	

奏 ソウ
R-1990

湊		ソウ		2309
R-2439	湊	みなと	harbor	

舛 シュン 瞬
↓ R-1585

舜		シュン		2915
R-2440	舜	むくげ	rose of Sharon; althea	
	舜	きよ	used in names	
	舜	ひとし	used in names	
	舜	よし	used in names	

厓 ガイ 涯
R-1385

崖		ガイ		2227
R-2441	断崖	ダンガイ	precipice	
	崖	がけ	cliff; bluff	

In the following groups, note that the signal primitive must stand in a dominant position—alone and to the right.

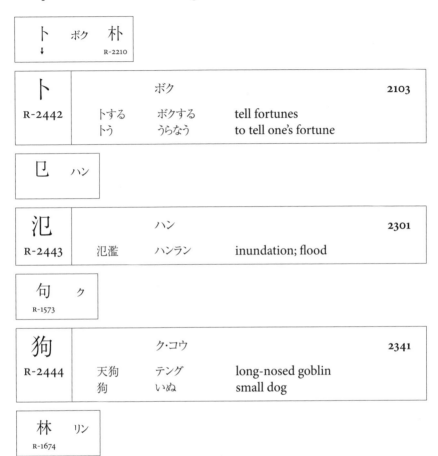

ト		ボク	朴
↓			R-2210

ト		ボク		2103
R-2442	トする	ボクする	tell fortunes	
	トう	うらなう	to tell one's fortune	

巴	ハン

氾		ハン		2301
R-2443	氾濫	ハンラン	inundation; flood	

句	ク
R-1573	

狗		ク・コウ		2341
R-2444	天狗	テング	long-nosed goblin	
	狗	いぬ	small dog	

林	リン
R-1674	

淋		リン		2310
R-2445	淋巴腺	リンパセン	lymph gland	
	淋しい	さびしい	lonely	

琳		リン		2554
R-2446	琳宇	リンウ	Taoist temple	

There are several new groups formed by picking up characters that were formerly part of pure or mixed groups. We take up these next.

梗		コウ・キョウ		2498
R-2447	梗塞	コウソク	stoppage; blockage	
	桔梗	キキョウ	Chinese bellflower	

便	ベン
R-865	

鞭		ベン		2783
R-2448	教鞭	キョウベン	teacher's rod	
	鞭	むち	whip	

凶	キョウ	胸	
R-866		R-867	

兇		キョウ		2853
R-2449	兇状	キョウジョウ	criminal offence	
	兇れる	おそれる	to fear	

This character was part of a semi-pure group in VOL. 2 but can best be learned here as a new group.

湯	トウ
R-1373	

蕩		トウ		2357
R-2450	蕩尽	トウジン	debauchee; libertine	
	蕩ける	とろける	be bewitched; be captivated	

This character was part of a mixed group in VOL. 2, but can best be learned here as a new group.

郭 カ ク R-1913			

廓 R-2451	カク		2235
	遊廓	ユウカク	licensed quarters
	廓	くるわ	licensed quarters

沙 サ ↓			

沙 R-2452	サ		2296
	無沙汰	ブサタ	neglect to call or write
	沙	すな	sand

裟 R-2453	サ		2701
	袈裟	ケサ	monk's surplice

离 リ 離 R-868			

璃 R-2454	リ		2048
	瑠璃	ルリ	lapis lazuli

丑 チュウ R-663			

紐 R-2455	チュウ		2661
	紐帯	チュウタイ	a band
	紐	ひも	string

希	キ
R-820	

稀		キ・ケ		**2611**
R-2456	稀薄	キハク	dilute	
	稀有	ケウ	rare; uncommon	
	稀	まれ	rare	

昏	コン	婚
↓		R-916

昏		コン		**2451**
R-2457	昏睡	コンスイ	coma	

脔	ダ	惰
		R-898

楕		ダ		**2531**
R-2458	楕円	ダエン	ellipse	

貝	バイ・ハイ
R-584	

唄		バイ・ハイ		**2178**
R-2459	唄讃	バイサン	song praising Buddhist virtues	

狽		バイ		**2340**
R-2460	狼狽	ロウバイ	panic	

幸 コウ R-1696				

倖 R-2461		コウ		**2119**
	倖い	さいわい	happy	

睾 R-2462		コウ		**2929**
	睾丸	コウガン	testicles	

連 レン R-1672				

蓮 R-2463		レン		**2360**
	蓮根	レンコン	lotus root	
	蓮	はちす	lotus	
	蓮	はす	lotus	

We conclude this chapter with entirely new pure groups—that is, those for whom neither the signal primitive nor any member of the group was introduced in VOL. 2. The number of these groups is small and should not cause much difficulty. Naturally, here the signal primitives stand alone in their small frames.

芻 スウ ↓				

芻 R-2464		スウ		**2084**
	反芻	ハンスウ	rumination	

趨 R-2465		スウ		**2086**
	趨地性	スウチセイ	geotropism	
	趨く	おもむく	head towards	

雛 R-2466	雛	スウ・ス ひな	chick	2085

耶 ↓	ヤ			

耶 R-2467	耶蘇 耶	ヤ ヤソ か	Jesus (old form) question mark	2680
爺 R-2468	爺 爺	ヤ じい じじ	old man old man; grandpa	2334
椰 R-2469	椰子 椰	ヤ ヤシ やし	palm tree palm tree	2524

冥 ↓	メイ			

冥 R-2470	冥王星 冥利	メイ・ミョウ メイオウセイ ミョウリ	Pluto (the planet) providence; divine favor	2841
瞑 R-2471	瞑想	メイ メイソウ	meditation	2842
暝 R-2472	暝天	メイ メイテン	Hades; underworld	2843

爾	ジ・ニ
↓	

爾		ジ・ニ		2074
R-2473	爾来	ジライ	since then	
	自然法爾	ジネンホウニ	"let it be" (Buddhist term)	
	爾	しか	only; in that manner	
	爾	なんじ	thou	
	爾	ちかし	used in names	

璽		ジ		2075
R-2474	国璽	コクジ	State Seal	

咢	ガク

顎		ガク		2795
R-2475	顎骨	ガッコツ	jawbone	
	顎	あご	jaw; chin	

鰐		ガク		2824
R-2476	鰐	わに	alligator	

晃	コウ
↓	

晃		コウ		2446
R-2477	晃	あき	used in names	
	晃	あきら	used in names	
	晃	てる	used in names	

滉 R-2478		コウ		2287
	滉	ひろ	used in names	
	滉	ひろし	used in names	
	Note that the character 幌 does not have a *kun-yomi* and has therefore not been included in this group.			

曳 ↓	エイ

曳 R-2479		エイ		2848
	曳光弾	エイコウダン	tracer bullet	
	曳く	ひく	to pull	
洩 R-2480		エイ・セツ		2849
	漏洩	ロウエイ	leak; disclosure	
	洩れ	もれ	to leak	

阜 ↓	フ

阜 R-2481		フ		2928
	岐阜県	ギフケン	prefecture in central Japan	
埠 R-2482		フ		2189
	埠頭	フトウ	wharf; pier; quay	

秦 ↓	シン

秦 R-2483		シン		2877
	秦代	シンダイ	Ch'in Dynasty (255–206 BCE)	
	秦	はた	used in family names	

榛		シン		2475
R-2484	榛	はしばみ	hazel tree	
	榛	はり	used in names	
	榛	はる	used in names	

豈	ガイ			

凱		ガイ		2077
R-2485	凱旋	ガイセン	triumphal return	
	凱	かちどき	used in names	
	凱らぐ	やわらぐ	victory cry	
	凱	とき	ease; be mitigated	
	凱	よし	used in names	

鎧		ガイ		2076
R-2486	鎧	よろい	suit of armor	

忽	コツ			
↓				

惚		コツ		2277
R-2487	恍惚	コウコツ	rapture; ecstasy	

忽		コツ		2431
R-2488	忽然	コツゼン	suddenly	
	忽ち	たちまち	all of a sudden	

刃	ジン			
R-2199				

靭		ジン		2786
R-2489	靭帯	ジンタイ	ligament; fascia	
	靭	うつぼ	quiver	

CHAPTER 9

Semi-Pure Groups

THE SEMI-PURE groups, it will be recalled from VOL. 2, are groups of *on-yomi* based on a common signal primitive—but with a single exception.

Strictly speaking, the addition of secondary and tertiary readings would do away with most semi-pure groups. But the classification is a useful one, and it is worth the strain to preserve it.

We begin here with semi-pure groups already learned, and conclude the chapter with a number of new groupings.

令 R-685	レイ	冷 R-686	零 R-687	鈴 R-688	齢 R-689	リョウ	領 R-690

苓 R-2490		レイ		2382
	苓北町	レイホクチョウ	town in Kumamoto Prefecture	
伶 R-2491		レイ		2112
	伶迅	レイジン	minstrel; court musician	
怜 R-2492		レイ		2278
	怜悧	レイリ	clever	
	怜い	さとい	wise	
	怜	さとし	used in names	
	怜	さと	used in names	
澪 R-2493		レイ		2285
	澪	みお	water canal	
玲 R-2494		レイ・リョウ		2568
	玲子	レイこ	Reiko (woman's name)	
	玲	あきら	used in names	
	玲	たま	used in names	

嶺 R-2495	レイ・リョウ		2228
	山嶺	サンレイ	peak
	嶺	みね	peak; summit
	Note that this character does *not*—as you would otherwise expect—follow the reading of the lower element, but keeps the reading of the signal primitive.		

粦	リン	隣	
		R-1980	

燐 R-2496	リン		2052
	燐酸	リンサン	phosphoric acid

鱗 R-2497	リン		2054
	鱗族	リンゾク	fish; finned family
	鱗	うろこ	fish scales
	鱗	こけ	fish scales

麟 R-2498	リン		2053
	麒麟	キリン	giraffe

憐 R-2499	レン		2051
	哀憐	アイレン	pity; compassion
	憐れむ	あわれむ	take pity

夋	シュン	俊	サ	唆	
		R-2074		R-2023	

峻 R-2500	シュン		2061
	峻拒	シュンキョ	flat refusal
	峻る	おわる	to be completed
	峻える	おえる	to complete
	峻	たか	used in names
	峻	たかし	used in names

悛	シュン		2059
R-2501	改悛 カイシュン	repentance	

竣	シュン		2062
R-2502	竣工 シュンコウ	completion of construction	

駿	シュン		2060
R-2503	駿馬 シュンメ	fleet steed	
	駿 たかし	used in names	
	駿 とし	used in names	
	駿 はやし	used in names	

交 コウ	校	効	郊	絞 カク	較	
R-671	R-672	R-673	R-674	R-675	R-676	

佼	コウ		2109
R-2504	立正佼成会 リッショウコウセイカイ	one of Japan's "new religions"	

狡	コウ		2337
R-2505	狡智 コウチ	crafty	
	狡い ずるい	cunning; sly	

枼 チョウ	蝶 ヨウ	葉	
	R-1885	R-1839	

喋	チョウ		2158
R-2506	喋々 チョウチョウ	long-winded	
	喋る しゃべる	to chatter	

牒	チョウ		2926
R-2507	符牒 フチョウ	mark; symbol; code	

諜	チョウ		2726
R-2508	防諜 ボウチョウ	counter-espionage	

瓜	カ	コ		弧	孤			
R-838				R-837	R-836			

菰			コ				2383
R-2509	菰	こも		water oat; matting rush			

狐			コ				2342
R-2510	狐狸	コリ		foxes and badgers			
	狐	きつね		fox			

辰	シン	震	娠	振	唇	ジョク	辱
R-730		R-731	R-732	R-733	R-734		R-735

賑			シン				2739
R-2511	賑やか	にぎやか		lively; cheerful; bustling			
	賑わう	にぎわう		flourish			

晨			シン				2443
R-2512	晨明	シンメイ		morning star			
	晨	あした		tomorrow			
	晨	あき		used in names			
	晨	とき		used in names			

并	ヘイ	併	塀	ビン	瓶	
		R-929	R-930		R-931	

屏			ヘイ・ビョウ				2223
R-2513	屏息	ヘイソク		bate one's breath			
	屏風	ビョウブ		Japanese folding screen			

餅			ヘイ				2802
R-2514	煎餅	センベイ		rice cracker			
	餅	もち		rice cake			

果	カ	課	菓	ラ	裸
R-760		R-761	R-762		R-763

夥		カ			2943
R-2515	夥しい	おびただしい	abundant		

意	オク	億	憶	イ	意
↗		R-854	R-855		R-856

臆		オク			2460
R-2516	臆病	オクビョウ	cowardice; timidity		

夫	フ	扶	キ	規	
R-824		R-825		R-826	

芙		フ			2361
R-2517	芙蓉	フヨウ	cotton rose		
	芙	はす	lotus		

奉	ホウ	俸	ボウ	棒	
R-797		R-798		R-799	

捧		ホウ			2265
R-2518	捧持	ホウジ	holding up; present		
	捧げる	さげる	to offer		

吉	キツ	詰	ケツ	結	
R-878		R-879		R-880	

桔		ケツ・キツ			2499
R-2519	桔梗	キキョウ	Chinese bellflower		

乍	サク	作	昨	酢	搾	サ	詐
		R-691	R-692	R-693	R-694		R-695

窄		サク		2614
R-2520	狭窄	キョウサク	constriction	
	窄む	すぼむ	constrict	
	窄む	つぼむ	to close up	

侖	リン	倫	輪	ロン	論
		R-899	R-900		R-901

綸		リン		2656
R-2521	綸言	リンゲン	Imperial edict (China)	
	綸	いと	satin cloth; used in names	
	綸	お	used in names	

骨	コツ	滑	カツ
R-422		R-423	

猾		カツ		2335
R-2522	狡猾	コウカツ	cunning	
	猾い	ずるい	sly	

圣	ケイ	経	軽	茎	径	カイ	怪
		R-720	R-721	R-722	R-723		R-724

頸		ケイ		2796
R-2523	頸動脈	ケイドウミャク	carotid artery	
	頸	くび	neck	

勁		ケイ		2990
R-2524	勁草	ケイソウ	hardy plants	
	勁い	つよい	sturdy	

Note that the primitive to the left is the old form of 圣. Another example appears in the following frame.

脛		ケイ		2989
R-2525	脛骨	ケイコツ	shinbone	
	脛	すね	shins	
	脛	はぎ	leg	

The following groups did not exist in VOL. 2, but can now be formed as semi-pure groups, using characters already known as signal primitives.

風	フウ
R-1070	

楓		フウ		2471
R-2526	楓子香	フウシコウ	galbanum (bitter gum resin)	
	楓	かえで	maple tree	

颯		サツ		2619
R-2527	颯爽	サッソウ	gallant; dashing	

刬	リュウ	留	ボウ	貿
		R-1691		R-1137

劉		リュウ		2143
R-2528	劉邦	リュウホウ	name of an Early Han-Dynasty emperor	

溜		リュウ		2324
R-2529	蒸溜	ジョウリュウ	distillation	
	溜める	ためる	store up	

瑠		リュウ・ル		2555
R-2530	瑠球	リュウキュウ	Loochoo Islands	
	瑠璃	ルリ	lapis lazuli	

夬	ケツ	決	カイ	快
		R-1602		R-1810

訣		ケツ		2714
R-2531	訣別	ケツベツ	parting; farewell	

抉		ケツ		2274
R-2532	抉出	ケッシュツ	gouging out	
	抉る	えぐる	gouge out	

委	イ
R-1706	

萎		イ		2355
R-2533	萎縮	イシュク	withering; atrophy	
	萎える	なえる	wither; droop	
	萎れる	しおれる	droop; be downcast	
	萎びる	しなびる	droop; wither	

倭		ワ		2106
R-2534	倭人	ワジン	name ancient Chinese used to refer to the Japanese	
	倭	かず	used in names	
	倭	ます	used in names	
	倭	しず	used in names	
	倭	やまと	Ancient Japan	

発	ハツ		ハイ	廃
R-1543				R-1554

溌		ハツ		2307
R-2535	溌剌	ハツラツ	sprightly; lively	

雚	カン	観	勧	歓	ケン・ゴン	権
		R-752	R-753	R-754		R-755

潅		カン		2314
R-2536	潅水	カンスイ	sprinkling; irrigation	

未	ミ	味	魅	マイ	妹
R-756		R-757	R-758		R-759

昧		マイ		2445
R-2537	愚昧	グマイ	stupidity; ignorance	

市	シ	姉	ハイ	肺
R-848		R-849		R-850

柿		シ		2481
R-2538	柿	かき	persimmon	

尊	ソン		ジュン	遵
R-1720				R-2181

樽		ソン		2506
R-2539	樽	たる	cask; keg	

鱒		ソン		2814
R-2540	鱒	ます	trout	

奇	キ	寄	騎
R-218		R-219	R-220

綺		キ		2667
R-2541	綺麗	キレイ	beautiful	
	綺	あや	used in names	

椅		イ		2480
R-2542	椅子	イス	chair	

旨	シ	指	脂
R-287		R-288	R-289

詣		ケイ		2715
R-2543	造詣	ゾウケイ	attainments; scholarship	

凡	ハン	帆
R-342		R-343

梵		ボン・ハン		2954
R-2544	梵語	ボンゴ	Sanskrit	

汎		ハン・ボン		2327
R-2545	汎神論	ハンシンロン	pantheism	

Note that *all* the characters allow for both readings. The divison indicates only "primary" reading.

弗	フツ	沸	ヒ	費
		R-2015		R-1643

狒		ヒ		2346
R-2546	狒々	ヒヒ	baboon	

屋	オク		アク	握
R-1820				R-1873

渥		アク		2320
R-2547	渥	あつ	used in names	
	渥	あつし	used in names	

The following group contains a final character that was classified in VOL. 2 as having no *on-yomi*. The secondary reading has, however, been added here for the sake of completeness.

責 R-764	セキ	積 R-765	績 R-766	サイ	債 R-767	シ	漬 R-641

蹟 R-2548	セキ		2743
	手蹟	シュセキ	handwriting specimen

巻 R-1791	カン		ケン	圏 R-2000

倦 R-2549	ケン		2108
	倦怠	ケンタイ	fatigue; weariness
	倦む	うむ	be untiring

尭 ↓	ギョウ	暁 R-2179	ショウ	焼 R-1681

尭 R-2550	ギョウ		2095
	尭	たか	used in names
	尭	たかし	used in names
	尭	ゆたか	used in names

莫 ↓	バク	漠 R-703	幕 R-702	マク	膜 R-701	幕 R-702	ボ	墓 R-696
		暮 R-697	模 R-698	募 R-699	慕 R-700			

莫 R-2551	バク		2105
	莫大	バクダイ	immense; colossal
	莫れ	なかれ	must not

危 キ		
R-1154		

跪	キ		2745
R-2552	跪坐 キザ	fall to one's knees	
	跪く ひざまずく	kneel down	

脆	ゼイ		2462
R-2553	脆性 ゼイセイ	brittleness; frailty	

旦 タン	胆	担	檀 チュウ	昼
R-715	R-716	R-717	R-718	R-719

坦	タン		2188
R-2554	平坦 ヘイタン	even; flat	

甘 カン	紺	
R-1909	R-1895	

嵌	カン		2229
R-2555	金象嵌 キンゾウガン	inlaying with gold	
	嵌める はめる	to inlay; set in; throw into	

柑	カン		2482
R-2556	蜜柑 ミカン	mandarin orange	

The following groups were introduced as pure groups in VOL. 2, but the addition of new characters makes them now semi-pure.

高 コウ	稿	
R-414	R-415	

膏	コウ		2923
R-2557	絆創膏 バンソウコウ	adhesive plaster (for wounds)	

嵩 R-2558		スウ		2224
	嵩	たかし	used in names	
	嵩	たか	used in names	

尉	イ	慰		
R-358		R-359		

蔚 R-2559		ウツ		2406
	蔚然	ウツゼン	growing luxuriantly	

盾	ジュン	循		
R-374		R-375		

楯 R-2560		ジュン		2513
	楯	たて	shield; escutcheon	

遁 R-2561		トン		2416
	遁辞	トンジ	excuse; subterfuge	

巨	キョ	拒	距	
R-224		R-225	R-226	

炬 R-2562		キョ・コ		2536
	炬火	キョカ	signal fire	
	炬	のり	used in names	

矩 R-2563		ク		2585
	矩形	クケイ	rectangle	

氏	テイ	低	抵	底	邸
		R-153	R-154	R-155	R-156

砥		シ			2590
R-2564	砥石	といし	grindstone; whetstone		

采	サイ	採	菜	彩
↓		R-242	R-243	R-244

采		サイ		2090
R-2565	采配	サイハイ	baton of command	
	采る	とる	take hold of	
	采	あや	used in names	
	采	うね	used in names	
	采	こと	used in names	

悉		シツ		2430
R-2566	知悉	チシツ	have full knowledge of	

Strictly speaking, the signal primitive does *not* appear in this kanji, but since 釆 is occasionally used in place of 采, we have included an example to draw attention to the difference.

氏	シ	紙
R-914		R-915

祇		ギ		2600
R-2567	祇園	ギオン	licenced quarters in Kyoto	

憂	ユウ	優
R-480		R-481

擾		ジョウ		2268
R-2568	擾乱	ジョウラン	riot; commotion	

申	シン	神	伸	紳
R-144		R-145	R-146	R-147

坤		コン		2184
R-2569	坤軸	コンジク	earth's axis (ancient China)	

比	ヒ	批
R-346		R-347

篦		ヘイ		2633
R-2570	竹篦	シッペイ	bamboo slat used to alert drowsy meditators	
	篦	へら	spatula	

虚	キョ		ギ	戯
R-1941				R-2082

嘘		キョ		2167
R-2571	嘘言	キョゲン	lie; falsehood	
	嘘	うそ	lie; falsehood	

朔	サク		ソ	塑
↓				R-2019

朔		サク		2846
R-2572	朔風	サクフウ	north wind	
	朔	ついたち	first day of the month	
	朔	はじめ	used in names	
	朔	もと	used in names	

遡		ソ		2847
R-2573	遡行	ソコウ	go against the stream	

念 ネン			
R-1114			

捻 R-2574		ネン	**2251**
	捻挫	ネンザ	sprain

稔 R-2575		ジン	**2607**
	稔熟	ジンジュク	fully ripened
	稔	とし	used in names
	稔	みのる	used in names
	稔	なり	used in names
	稔	なる	used in names

In the following group, the signal primitive must stand alone and to the right. We have seen in other cases as well how certain primitives, in order to serve as a *signal primitive*, must be in a *dominant position*.

全 ゼン		セン 栓	
R-989		R-1759	

詮 R-2576		セン	**2717**
	詮索	センサク	search; exploration

朝 チョウ 潮			
R-330	R-331		

廟 R-2577		ビョウ	**2239**
	廟堂	ビョウドウ	court; ministry

嘲 R-2578		チョウ	**2155**
	嘲弄	チョウロウ	mockery; ridicule
	嘲る	あざける	to make fun of

旬	ジュン	殉
R-372		R-373

詢		ジュン・シュン		2705
R-2579	諮詢	シジュン	consultation; inferring	
	詢る	はかる	consult	
	詢	まこと	used in names	

洵		シュン・ジュン		2290
R-2580	洵涕	ジュンテイ	weeping silently	
	洵	まこと	used in names	

絢		ケン		2664
R-2581	絢爛	ケンラン	dazzling; gorgeous; gaudy	
	絢	あや	used in names	

Finally, there are a small number of entirely new semi-pure groups, composed only of kanji learned in this volume.

奄	アン ・ エン
↓	

庵		アン		2056
R-2582	庵室	アンシツ	hermit's cell	
	庵	いおり	hermitage	

奄		エン		2055
R-2583	気息奄々	キソクエンエン	gasp for breath; huff and puff	

掩		エン		2057
R-2584	掩蔽	エンペイ	cover; obscuration	
	掩う	おおう	to cover	

俺		エン		2058
R-2585	俺	おれ	me	

畏 イ				
↓				

隈		ワイ		2427
R-2586	界隈	カイワイ	neighborhood; vicinity	

猥		ワイ		2336
R-2587	猥雑	ワイザツ	indecency; lewdness	
	猥ら	みだら	loose	

畏		イ		2569
R-2588	畏縮	イシュク	wince; flinch	

咠 シュウ				

葺		シュウ		2392
R-2589	葺く	ふく	to thatch; shingle	

輯		シュウ		2732
R-2590	輯録	シュウロク	compilation; editing	

揖		ユウ・シュウ		2263
R-2591	揖拝	ユウハイ	bowing with arms folded	

它 ダ ジャ 蛇				

舵		ダ		2674
R-2592	舵輪	ダリン	steering wheel; helm	

	舵	かじ	rudder; helm	
陀 R-2593		ダ		2955
	仏陀	ブッダ	Buddha	
詫 R-2594		タ		2718
	詫く	あざむく	dupe; deceive	

雁 ↓	ガン・ヨウ

贋 R-2595		ガン		2151
	贋造	ガンゾウ	counterfeit	
雁 R-2596		ガン		2150
	雁行	ガンコウ	side by side, like flying geese	
鷹 R-2597		ヨウ		2237
	鷹	たか	hawk	

因 R-905	イン	姻 R-906	オン	恩 R-907	

咽 R-2598		イン		2159
	咽喉	インコウ	throat	
	咽	のど	throat	

The following group was not learned as a pure group in VOL. 2, but if its signal primitive is made to stand alone and on the right, it is convenient to make the group now.

里	リ	鯉	理	マイ	埋
R-1160		R-590	R-963		R-1995

		リ		2951
浬				
R-2599	三浬	サンリ	three nautical miles	

		リ		2338
狸				
R-2600	狐狸	コリ	foxes and badgers	
	狸	たぬき	badger-dog	

		リ		2950
哩				
R-2601	五哩	ゴリ	five miles	
	哩	マイル	mile	

		リ		2973
裡				
R-2602	裡面	リメン	back side	
	裡	うら	behind (old form)	

良	リョウ		ロウ	朗	浪
R-892				R-890	R-891

		ロウ		2339
狼				
R-2603	狼星	ロウセイ	Sirius; Dog Star	
	狡い	こすい	sly; cunning	

胡	コ	湖
↓		R-1216

		コ		2650
糊				
R-2604	糊塗	コト	makeshift	
	糊	のり	paste; glue	

胡 R-2605		コ・ゴ・ウ		2470
	胡椒	コショウ	pepper	
	胡麻	ゴマ	sesame	
	胡乱	ウロン	suspicious-looking	
	胡	えびす	barbarians	
	胡	ひさ	used in names	
瑚 R-2606		ゴ・コ		2562
	珊瑚	サンゴ	coral	
醐 R-2607		ゴ		2749
	醍醐味	ダイゴミ	zest for life	

The following group was learned as a pure group in VOL. 2, but the primary reading of the signal primitive makes it better to reclassify it as a semi-pure group.

無 R-324	ム・ブ

撫 R-2608		ブ		2270
	撫養	ブヨウ	care; tending	
	撫でる	なでる	to stroke; pet	
蕪 R-2609		ブ		2401
	蕪雑	ブザツ	unpolished; crude	
	蕪	かぶ	turnip	

屯 R-2188	トン		ジュン	純 R-1991		ドン	鈍 R-2071

沌 R-2610		トン		2326
	混沌	コントン	chaos; confusion	

頓		トン		2788
R-2611	頓智	トンチ	ready wit	

嚬		トン		2949
R-2612	嚬	トン	a ton	

玄	コウ	ユウ 雄		
		R-1918		

宏		コウ		2212
R-2613	宏大	コウダイ	vast; extensive	
	宏	あつ	used in names	
	宏	ひろ	used in names	
	宏	ひろし	used in names	

紘		コウ		2662
R-2614	八紘一宇	ハッコウイチウ	"everything under one roof"	
	紘	ひろ	used in names	
	紘	ひろし	used in names	

肱		コウ		2469
R-2615	股肱	ココウ	right-hand man	
	肱	ひじ	elbow	

It happens occasionally, as in the following group, that the signal primitive forms an exception to the reading it takes in other characters in which it appears.

前	ゼン
R-1012	

煎		セン		2548
R-2616	煎餅	センベイ	rice cracker	
	煎る	いる	to roast	

箭		セン		2636
R-2617	箭書	センショ	message attached to an arrow	
	箭	や	arrow	
剪		セン		2941
R-2618	剪定	センテイ	pruning	
揃		セン		2255
R-2619	揃える	そろえる	to assemble; muster	

CHAPTER 10

Mixed Groups

THE 162 KANJI treated in this chapter make up the most difficult of the signal-primitive-based groups. Let us begin by recalling the three classes of "mixed groups" introduced in Vol. 2:

GROUP A includes groups with two readings. As distinct from the "semi-pure" groups, there must be at least 2 kanji for each reading.

Group B is made up of groups with only two exceptions to the standard reading of the signal primitive, which must apply to at least 3 kanji.

Group C is made up of miscellaneous groups where it is still useful to see a signal primitive with a standard reading, but which has exceptions other than those that apply to Groups A and B.

With the addition of so many new kanji in this volume, several of the groups from VOL. 2 will change classification. What is more, once we have left the confines of the readings assigned for "general use," the number of secondary and tertiary *on-yomi* increases dramatically, making the distinction between Group A and Group B less useful. Accordingly, the two groups have been combined in the present volume. For further information on the layout of the frames, see the opening remarks to Chapter 7 and the full diagram on page 8.

GROUPS A & B

卑	ヒ	碑		
R-348		R-349		

痺		ヒ		2579
R-2620	麻痺	マヒ	paralysis	
	痺れる	しびれる	go numb	

婢	ヒ		2196
R-2621	奴婢 ヌヒ	servants	

牌	ハイ		2873
R-2622	賞牌 ショウハイ	medallion	
	牌 パイ	mah-jong tiles (Chinese)	

稗	ハイ		2608
R-2623	稗史 ハイシ	legend; fiction	
	稗 ひえ	barnyard grass	

辟 ヘキ 壁 癖 ヒ 避
R-851 R-852 R-853

僻	ヘキ		2117
R-2624	僻見 ヘキケン	prejudice	
	僻む ひがむ	be biased against	

譬	ヒ		2728
R-2625	譬喩 ヒユ	metaphor	
	譬える たとえる	compare; liken to	

肖 ショウ 消 硝 宵 サク 削
R-725 R-726 R-727 R-728 R-729

鞘	ショウ		2784
R-2626	鞘 さや	a sheath	

哨	ショウ		2154
R-2627	哨戒 ショウカイ	patrol; guard	

屑	セツ		2219
R-2628	屑 くず	waste; rubbish	

比	ヒ	批		
R-346		R-347		

庇		ヒ		2236
R-2629	庇護	ヒゴ	aegis; protection	
	庇う	かばう	protect; grant sanctuary	
	庇	ひさし	eaves; canopy	

屁		ヒ		2218
R-2630	放屁	ホウヒ	breaking wind	
	屁	へ	passed gas	

枇		ビ		2519
R-2631	枇杷	ビワ	loquat	

琵	·	ビ		2912
R-2632	琵琶	ビワ	lute	

夗	エン	苑	怨	宛	ワン	腕
		R-780	R-781	R-782		R-783

椀		ワン		2487
R-2633	椀	ワン	wooden bowl	

碗		ワン		2591
R-2634	茶碗	チャワン	teacup	

婉		エン		2197
R-2635	婉曲	エンキョク	euphemistic	

般	ハン	搬	バン	盤
R-800		R-801		R-802

槃		ハン		2522
R-2636	涅槃	ネハン	nirvana	

磐		バン		2586
R-2637	磐石	バンジャク	huge rock	
	磐	いわ	boulder	

監	カン	艦	鑑	ラン	濫
R-748		R-749	R-750		R-751

藍		ラン		2371
R-2638	伽藍	ガラン	temple for Buddhist training	
	藍	あい	indigo	

弟	ダイ	第	デ	弟	テイ	弟
R-544		R-1416		↗		↗

剃		テイ		2146
R-2639	剃髪	テイハツ	tonsure; cutting off the hair	
	剃る	そる	to shave	

悌		テイ		2283
R-2640	悌順	テイジュン	obedience	
	悌	とも	used in names	
	悌	よし	used in names	
	悌	やす	used in names	
	悌	やすし	used in names	

梯		テイ		2479
R-2641	階梯	カイテイ	step; threshold; guide	
	梯	はしご	ladder	

兼	レン	廉	鎌	ケン	兼	謙	嫌	ゲン	嫌
↗		R-1202	R-1203		R-1199	R-1200	R-1201		R-1201

簾		レン						2630
R-2642	暖簾	ノレン			shop-entrance curtain			
	簾	すだれ			bamboo blind			

某	ボウ	謀	バイ	媒
R-806		R-807		R-808

煤		バイ				2541
R-2643	煤煙	バイエン		soot and smoke		
	煤	すす		soot		

正	ショウ	政	証	症	セイ	正	政	整	征
↗		R-1205	R-1208	R-1209		R-1204	R-1205	R-1206	R-1207

鉦		ショウ				2770
R-2644	鉦鼓	ショウコ		a bell and drum		
	鉦	かね		bell clapper		

兆	チョウ	跳	挑	眺	トウ	桃	逃
R-1168		R-1169	R-1170	R-1171		R-1172	R-1173

銚		チョウ		2755
R-2645	銚子	チョウシ	saké holder	

曽	ソウ	層	僧	贈	ゾウ	増	憎	贈	ソ	曽
↗		R-1188	R-1189	R-1193		R-1191	R-1192	R-1193		R-1190

噌		ソ			2177
R-2646	味噌	ミソ	fermented bean paste		

成	ジョウ	盛	城	セイ	成	盛	誠
R-1174		R-1175	R-1177		R-1174	R-1175	R-1176

晟	ジョウ		2438
R-2647	晟らか あきらか	clear	
	晟 あきら	used in names	

右	ユウ・ウ
R-1754	

佑	ウ・ユウ		2126
R-2648	天佑 テンユウ	divine favor; providence	
	佑 すけ	used in names	
	佑く たすく	aid; assist	

祐	ユウ		2599
R-2649	祐筆 ユウヒツ	secretary; amanuensis	
	祐 さち	used in names	
	祐 すけ	used in names	
	祐 たすく	used in names	
	祐 ち	used in names	
	祐 ます	used in names	

干	カン	幹	刊	汗	肝	ケン	軒	ガン	岸
R-1270		R-1269	R-1271	R-1272	R-1273		R-1274		R-1275

鼾	カン		2944
R-2650	鼾声 カンセイ	snoring voice	
	鼾 いびき	snoring	

旱	カン		2441
R-2651	旱害 カンガイ	drought damage	
	旱 ひでり	drought	

竿 R-2652		カン		2632
	竿頭	カントウ	top of a pole	
	竿	さお	pole	

栞 R-2653		カン		2523
	栞	しおり	bookmark	

台 タイ	怠	胎 ジ・チ	治 シ	始
R-1264	R-1265	R-1266	R-1267	R-1268

冶 R-2654		ヤ		2137
	陶冶	トウヤ	training; cultivation	

殆 R-2655		タイ		2871
	殆ど	ほとんど	almost	

苔 R-2656		タイ		2356
	蘇苔	センタイ	mosses	
	苔	こけ	moss	
	海苔	のり	seaweed	

古 コ	枯	故 ク	苦 キョ	居
R-1215	R-1218	R-1217	R-1219	R-1220

姑 R-2657		コ		2205
	姑息	コソク	stopgap; makeshift	
	姑	しゅうと	mother-in-law	
	姑	しゅうとめ	mother-in-law	

反 ハン 坂 板 販 版 阪 飯 バン 板
R-1234　　　R-1233　R-1235　R-1236　R-1237　R-1238　R-1239　　　R-1235

タン 反 ヘン 返 カ 仮 ホン 反
　　R-1234　　　R-1240　　　R-1241　　　R-1234

叛		ホン・ハン			2902
R-2658	謀叛	ムホン	rebellion; insurrection		
	叛く	そむく	disobey		

戔 セン 浅 銭 践 サン 桟 ザン 残
　　　　　R-1259　R-1260　R-1261　　　R-1262　　　R-1263

箋		セン		2991
R-2659	便箋	ビンセン	letter paper	

賤		セン		2735
R-2660	貴賤	キセン	high and low (social rank)	
	賤しい	いやしい	lowly; humble	

韋 イ 違 偉 緯 エイ 衛 カン 韓
　　　R-1221　R-1222　R-1223　　　R-1224　　　R-1225

葦		イ		2411
R-2661	葦	あし	reeds	
	葦	よし	reeds	

曷 カツ 喝 褐 渇 エツ 謁 ケイ 掲
　　　R-1210　R-1211　R-1212　　　R-1213　　　R-1214

葛		カツ		2398
R-2662	葛藤	カットウ	confrontation; discord	
	葛	くず	kudzu; arrowroot	

其	キ	旗	棋	基	期	ギ	欺	ゴ	碁
		R-1253	R-1254	R-1255	R-1256		R-1257		R-1258

箕		キ		2643
R-2663	簸箕	ハキ	winnowing fan	
	箕	み	winnow; winnowing fan	

麒		キ		2840
R-2664	麒麟	キリン	giraffe	

合	コウ	カッ・ガッ・ゴウ	合	シュウ・ジュウ	拾
↗			R-1074		R-1813

恰		コウ・カッ		2281
R-2665	恰好	カッコウ	shape; form	
	恰も	あたかも	as if	

閤		コウ		2776
R-2666	太閤	タイコウ	father of the Imperial adviser	

牙	ガ	芽	雅	ジャ	邪
R-784		R-785	R-786		R-787

冴		コ・ゴ		2134
R-2667	冴え	さえ	intelligent; bright	
	冴える	さえる	be clear; serene	

定	テイ	ジョウ	定	錠
↗			R-360	R-361

碇		テイ		2587
R-2668	碇泊地	テイハクチ	anchorage; mooring	
	碇	いかり	anchor	

綻		タン		2670
R-2669	破綻	ハタン	failure; bankruptcy	
	綻びる	ほころびる	unravel	

此	シ	紫	雌	
↓		R-522	R-523	

此		シ		2043
R-2670	此岸	シガン	this shore (this world)	
	此	これ	this one	

柴		サイ		2044
R-2671	柴	しば	brushwood	

砦		サイ		2045
R-2672	城砦	ジョウサイ	fort; citadel	
	砦	とりで	fort; fortifications	

些		サ		2046
R-2673	些細	ササイ	trifling; trivial	
	些か	いささか	slightly	
	些し	すこし	small amount	

享	キョウ
R-1828	

淳		ジュン		2318
R-2674	淳心	ジュンシン	pure and immaculate heart	
	淳	あつ	used in names	
	淳	あつし	used in names	
	淳	あき	used in names	
	淳	きよ	used in names	
	淳	きよし	used in names	
	淳	まこと	used in names	

醇		ジュン		2751
R-2675	醇化	ジュンカ	refinement; sublimation	
	醇い	あつい	warm; cordial	
	醇	あつ	used in names	
	醇	あつし	used in names	

惇		ジュン・トン		2279
R-2676	惇い	あつい	warm; cordial	
	惇	あつし	used in names	
	惇	まこと	used in names	

敦		トン		2931
R-2677	敦厚	トンコウ	simplicity; naivete	
	敦	あつし	used in names	
	敦	あつ	used in names	
	敦	つる	used in names	
	敦	のぶ	used in names	
	敦	おさむ	used in names	
	敦	つとむ	used in names	

分	フン	粉	紛	雰	ボン	盆
		R-1247	R-1248	R-1249		R-1250

	ヒン・ビン	貧	ハン	頒	ブン・ブ	分
		R-1251		R-1252		R-1246

扮		フン		2246
R-2678	扮装	フンソウ	get-up; disguise	

垂	スイ	睡	錘	ユウ	郵
R-736		R-737	R-738		R-739

唾		ダ		2165
R-2679	唾液	ダエキ	saliva; sputum	

GROUP C

甫	ホ	舗	補	浦	捕	フ	蒲
↓		R-61	R-62	R-63	R-64		R-650

葡		ブ・ホ		2378
R-2680	葡萄	ブドウ	grape; grapevine	

輔		ホ・フ		2730
R-2681	輔佐	ホサ	assistant; counselor	
	輔	すけ	used in names	
	輔く	たすく	to help; assist	

甫		ホ		2097
R-2682	甫	ひろし	used in names	
	甫	はじめ	used in names	

舗		ホ		2975
R-2683	舗道	ホドウ	paved road	

圃		ホ		2918
R-2684	圃畦	ホケイ	ridges in fields	

加	カ	架	ガ	賀
R-788		R-789		R-790

伽		カ・ガ		2115
R-2685	伽陀	カダ	song in praise of the Buddha (gatha)	
	伽藍	ガラン	temple; monastery	
	伽	とぎ	nursing	

嘉 R-2686		カ		2852
	嘉納	カノウ	approval; appreciation	
	嘉す	よみす	praise as good	
	嘉	よし	used in names	
	嘉	ひろ	used in names	

茄 R-2687		カ		2372
	茄(子)	なす	eggplant	

迦 R-2688		カ		2959
	釈迦	シャカ	Shakyamuni the Buddha	

珈 R-2689		カ		2962
	珈琲	コーヒー	coffee	

駕 R-2690		カ・ガ		2803
	駕籠	カゴ	palanquin; litter	
	車駕	シャガ	imperial carriage	

袈 R-2691		ケ		2700
	袈裟	ケサ	monk's surplice	

真 R-923	シン	慎 R-924	チン	鎮 R-925

槙 R-2692		テン		2492
	槙	まき	Chinese black pine	

顛 R-2693		テン		2789
	顛末	テンマツ	details; full account	

填 R-2694		テン		2190
	填補	テンポ	fill up; compensate for	

戈	サイ	裁	載	栽	セン	繊
		R-740	R-741	R-742		R-743

		サイ		2704
哉 R-2695	快哉	カイサイ	shout of delight	
	哉	か	question mark; used in names	
	哉	かな	indeed; used in names	
	哉	ちか	used in names	
	哉	はじめ	used in names	
	哉	や	used in names	

		セツ		2703
截 R-2696	截然	セツゼン	distinct; sharp	
	截る	きる	sever; cut	

		タイ		2702
戴 R-2697	頂戴	チョウダイ	accept; receive	

生	セイ・ショウ	姓	性	星	セイ	牲	サン	産
R-1281		R-1282	R-1283	R-1284		R-1286		R-1285

		セイ		2750
醒 R-2698	覚醒剤	カクセイザイ	stimulant; drug	
	醒ます	さます	to wake someone	

		セイ		2910
甥 R-2699	甥	おい	nephew	

		ショウ		2628
笙 R-2700	笙鼓	ショウコ	flutes and drums	
	笙	しょうのふえ	13- or 19-reed pan flute	

甦		ソ			2940
R-2701	甦生 甦る	ソセイ よみがえる	resuscitation; rebirth revive; resucitate		

告	コク	酷	ゾウ	造
R-926		R-927		R-928

皓		コウ			2934
R-2702	皓歯 皓 皓	コウシ あきら ひろし	pearly-white teeth used in names used in names		

畐	フク	福	副	幅	フ	富
		R-744	R-745	R-746		R-747

輻		フク			2731
R-2703	輻射 輻	フクシャ や	radiation (of heat, light, etc.) spoke of a wheel		

逼		ヒツ			2420
R-2704	逼塞	ヒッソク	dropping out of the picture after a failure		

艮	コン	根	恨	ゲン	限	眼	ガン	眼
		R-1396	R-1397		R-1398	R-1399		R-1399
	ギン	銀	タイ	退				
		R-1400		R-1401				

痕		コン			2578
R-2705	痕跡 痕	コンセキ あと	traces; vestiges scar		

丁	テイ	訂	チョウ	丁	町	頂	庁	チョ	貯
↗	R-1464		R-1458	R-1459	R-1460	R-1461			R-1462

	トウ	灯	ダ	打
		R-1463		R-1465

汀		テイ		2312
R-2706	汀線	テイセン	beach line	
	汀	なぎさ	beach	
	汀	みぎわ	waterside	

釘		テイ		2766
R-2707	装釘	ソウテイ	book-binding	
	釘	くぎ	nail	

直	ショク	殖	植	チ	値	置	チョク・ジキ	直
R-1325		R-1323	R-1324		R-1321	R-1322		R-1325

埴		ショク		2183
R-2708	埴	はに	clay	

東	レン	練	錬	トウ	東	凍	チン	陳
↗		R-1328	R-1329		R-1326	R-1327		R-1330

煉		レン		2542
R-2709	煉瓦	レンガ	brick	
	煉る	ねる	temper; soften	

諫		カン		2708
R-2710	諫言	カンゲン	admonition	
	諫める	いさめる	remonstrate	

舌 ◢	カツ	活 R-1500	括 R-1501	ゼツ	舌 R-1502	ワ	話 R-1503
	ジ	辞 R-1504	ケイ	憩 R-1505			

筈 R-2711			カツ		2646
	筈	はず		expectation; should	

区 R-1470	ク R-1471	駆	オウ R-1472	欧 R-1473	殴	スウ	枢 R-1474

躯 R-2712		ク		2986
	老躯	ロウク	old bones; advanced age	
	躯	からだ	body	

鴎 R-2713		オウ		2828
	鴎	かもめ	seagull	

音 ◢	アン	暗 R-1301	イン	韻 R-1299	音 R-1300	オン	音 R-1300

闇 R-2714		アン		2777
	諒闇	リョウアン	court (national) mourning	
	闇	やみ	darkness	
	闇い	くらい	dark; shadowy	

寺 R-1433	ジ	持 R-1434	侍 R-1435	時 R-1436	シ	詩 R-1437	タイ	待 R-1438
	トウ	等 R-1439	トク	特 R-1440				

痔 R-2715		ジ		2575
	痔	ジ	hemorrhoids	

蒔		ジ		**2395**
R-2716	蒔く	まく	to sow	
	蒔える	うえる	to plant	
	蒔	まき	used in names	

非	ヒ	悲	扉	ハイ	俳	輩	排	ザイ	罪
R-1429		R-1430	R-1431		R-1426	R-1427	R-1428		R-1432

斐		ヒ		**2897**
R-2717	斐川町	ヒかわチョウ	town in Shimane Prefecture	
	斐	あや	used in names	
	生甲斐	いきがい	reason for living	

緋		ヒ		**2659**
R-2718	緋鯉	ヒごい	red (gold) carp	
	緋	あか	red	
	緋	あけ	red; crimson	

誹		ヒ		**2724**
R-2719	誹謗	ヒボウ	slander; calumny	
	誹る	そしる	accuse; slander	

琲		ハイ・ヒ		**2963**
R-2720	珈琲	コーヒー	coffee	

皮	ヒ	被	彼	疲	披	ハ	破	波
R-1418		R-1419	R-1420	R-1421	R-1422		R-1423	R-1424
	バ	婆						
		R-1425						

頗		ハ		**2793**
R-2721	偏頗	ヘンパ	partiality; favoritism	
	頗る	すこぶる	exceedingly; extremely	

簸		ハ		2647
R-2722	簸箕	ハキ	winnowing fan	

免	バン	晩	イツ	逸	ベン	勉	メン	免
ノ		R-949		R-1868		R-952		R-1117

挽		バン		2244
R-2723	挽歌	バンカ	eulogy; dirge	
	挽く	ひく	grind (meat)	

禺	グウ	偶	遇	隅	グ	愚
		R-776	R-777	R-778		R-779

寓		グウ		2211
R-2724	寓話	グウワ	allegory; fable	

萬		マン		2969
R-2725	弐萬	ニマン	20,000 (old form)	

邁		マイ		2970
R-2726	高邁	コウマイ	lofty; noble	

豆	トウ	痘	闘	登	頭	ト	登	頭
ノ		R-1442	R-1443	R-1444	R-1445		R-1444	R-1445
	ズ	豆	頭	ホウ	豊	チョウ	澄	タン	短
		R-1441	R-1445		R-1446		R-1447		R-1448

逗		トウ・ズ		2423
R-2727	逗留	トウリュウ	stayover; sojourn	
	逗子市	ズシシ	city near Kamakura	

翟	ヨウ	曜	ヤク	躍	タク	濯
		R-976		R-2076		R-2208

耀		ヨウ		2880
R-2728	耀く	かがやく	shine; sparkle	
	耀	あきら	used in names	
	耀	てる	used in names	

燿		ヨウ		2534
R-2729	燿く	かがやく	shine brightly	
	燿	てる	used in names	

番	バン・ハン	藩
R-948		R-2152

蕃		バン		2381
R-2730	蕃椒	バンショウ	red pepper	

播		ハ		2262
R-2731	播種	ハシュ	sowing; planting	
	播く	まく	to sow	

昜	ヨウ	陽	揚	チョウ	腸	トウ	湯
		R-1370	R-1371		R-1372		R-1373
	ジョウ	場	ショウ	傷			
		R-1374		R-1375			

暢		チョウ		2885
R-2732	流暢	リュウチョウ	fluent (in speaking)	
	暢	いたる	used in names	
	暢	かど	used in names	
	暢	とおる	used in names	
	暢	なが	used in names	
	暢	のぶ	used in names	

	暢	まさ	used in names	
	暢	みつ	used in names	
楊		ヨウ		2473
R-2733	楊枝	ヨウジ	toothpick	
	楊	やす	used in names	
	楊	やなぎ	willow	

Note similarities in the following kanji that seem to create "pure" groups in an otherwise mixed group by adding a second element.

者	ショ	署	暑	諸	渚	緒	シャ	者	煮
'		R-1362	R-1363	R-1364	R-629	R-1367		R-1360	R-1361
	チョ	著	猪	緒	ト	都	賭	ツ	都
		R-1365	R-1366	R-1367		R-1368	R-1369		R-1368

曙		ショ		2448
R-2734	曙光	ショコウ	first light of dawn	
	曙	あけぼの	dawn; daybreak	
	曙	あきら	used in names	
薯		ショ		2365
R-2735	甘薯	カンショ	sweet potato	
	薯	いも	potato	
藷		ショ		2402
R-2736	甘藷	カンショ	sweet potato	
	藷	いも	potato	
躇		チョ		2994
R-2737	躊躇	チュウチョ	hesitation; warning	

儲		チョ		2118
R-2738	儲利	チョリ	profits; earnings	
	儲け	もうけ	profits	
	儲ける	もうける	make a profit	

堵		ト		2192
R-2739	安堵	アンド	feeling of relief	

屠		ト		2217
R-2740	屠場	トジョウ	slaughterhouse	
	屠る	ほふる	defeat	

各	ラク	絡	落	酪	カク	各	格	閣	客
＇		R-1355	R-1356	R-1357		R-1351	R-1352	R-1353	R-1354
	リャク	略	ガク	額	キャク	客			
		R-1358		R-1359		R-1354			

洛		ラク		2302
R-2741	洛中	ラクチュウ	in Kyoto	

烙		ラク		2545
R-2742	烙印	ラクイン	branding; stigma	
	烙く	やく	to burn	

賂		ロ		2738
R-2743	賄賂	ワイロ	bribe	

In the following group, the primitive must stand alone and on the right to qualify as a signal primitive.

京	リョウ	涼	キョウ・ケイ	京	ゲイ	鯨
✦		R-2177		R-938		R-1917

掠		リャク		**2247**
R-2744	掠奪	リャクダツ	pillage; looting	
	掠める	かすめる	to plunder; loot	

椋		リョウ		**2474**
R-2745	椋	むくのき	gray starling	
	椋	くら	used in names	

諒		リョウ		**2710**
R-2746	諒闇	リョウアン	court (national) mourning	
	諒	まこと	used in names	
	諒	さとし	used in names	

若	ジャク	トク	匿	ダク	諾
R-1962			R-2190		R-1760

惹		ジャク		**2429**
R-2747	惹起	ジャッキ	provocation	
	惹く	ひく	to attract; solicit	

圭	ケイ	桂	カ	佳	ガイ	街	涯
R-1387		R-1386		R-1388		R-1384	R-1385
	カイ	街	フウ・ホウ	封			
		R-1384		R-1389			

奎		ケイ		**2932**
R-2748	奎	ふみ	used in names	

畦		ケイ		2571
R-2749	畦	あぜ	ridge between rice fields	
	畦	うね	ridge; furrow	

鮭		ケイ		2815
R-2750	鮭	さけ	salmon	

珪		ケイ		2564
R-2751	珪素	ケイソ	silicon	

蛙		ア		2693
R-2752	蛙声	アセイ	raucous voice	
	蛙	かえる	a frog	

娃		アイ		2200
R-2753	娃しい	うつくしい	beautiful	

支	シ	枝	肢	ギ	技	キ	岐
R-1402		R-1403	R-1404		R-1405		R-1406

伎		ギ・キ		2122
R-2754	伎芸	ギゲイ	arts; handicrafts	
	歌舞伎	カブキ	Kabuki	
	伎	わぎ	used in names	
	伎	くれ	used in names	

妓		ギ		2199
R-2755	妓楼	ギロウ	brothel	

This next group of characters, you may recall, was given special attention in VOL. 2 because of the overlap of readings. Having come this far already, it is no doubt clear to you that this exception has become rather the rule in VOL. 3.

戠	シキ	識	織	ショク	職	織
		R-932	R-934		R-933	R-934

幟	シ		2233
R-2756	旗幟　キシ	flag; banner; one's position	
	幟　のぼり	a banner; a streamer	

羊	ヨウ	洋	様	養	窯	ショウ	祥	詳
R-1449		R-1450	R-1451	R-1452	R-1453		R-1454	R-1455
	セン	鮮	ミ・ビ	美				
		R-1456		R-1457				

痒	ヨウ		2572
R-2757	痛痒　ツウヨウ	itching; interest	
	痒い　かゆい	itchy	

軍	キ	揮	輝	グン	軍	ウン	運
↗		R-1520	R-1521		R-1522		R-1523

暈	ウン		2439
R-2758	眩暈　ゲンウン	vertigo; dizziness	
	暈　かさ	halo	
	暈す　ぼかす	shade off; blur	
	暈ける　ぼける	fade; grow dim	

渾	コン		2295
R-2759	渾天儀　コンテンギ	astrolabe	

暉	キ		2440
R-2760	暉き　かがやき	a glow	
	暉る　てる	to glow	
	暉　ひかり	ray of light	
	暉　あきら	used in names	
	暉　てる	used in names	

主	チュウ	注	柱	駐	シュ・ス	主	
✓		R-1331	R-1332	R-1333		R-1335	
	ジュウ	住	オウ	往			
		R-1336		R-1337			

註		チュウ		2727
R-2761	註釈	チュウシャク	annotate	

巴	ハ	把	ヒ	肥
↓		R-2083		R-1618

巴		ハ		2096
R-2762	淋巴腺	リンパセン	lymph glands	
	巴	うず	a swirl	
	巴	ともえ	used in names	

琶		ハ		2913
R-2763	琵琶	ビワ	Japanese lute	

芭		バ		2386
R-2764	芭蕉	バショウ	Bashō (haiku poet); banana	

杷		ワ		2501
R-2765	枇杷	ビワ	loquat	

周	チョウ	調	彫	シュウ	周	週
✓		R-1531	R-1532		R-1533	R-1534

凋		チョウ		2135
R-2766	凋落	チョウラク	withering; decline	
	凋む	しぼむ	wither	

鯛		チョウ		2812
R-2767	鯛	たい	sea bream	

亥	ガイ	該	劾	カク	核	コク	刻
R-640		R-1535	R-1536		R-1537		R-1538

咳		ガイ		2162
R-2768	咳唾	ガイダ	cough and spittle	
	咳	せき	cough	

骸		ガイ		2874
R-2769	屍骸	シガイ	corpse	

也	チ	地	池	ジ	地	シ・セ	施	タ	他
↓		R-1287	R-1288		R-1287		R-1289		R-1291

也		ヤ		2094
R-2770	也	なり	to the amount of (on receipts)	
	也	あり	used in names	
	也	また	used in names	

弛		チ・シ		2242
R-2771	弛緩	チカン・シカン	relaxation; slackening	
	弛張	シチョウ	tightening and loosening	
	弛む	たるむ	slacken	
	弛む	ゆるむ	slacken	

馳		チ		2805
R-2772	馳走	チソウ	treat; hospitality	
	馳せる	はせる	run; gallop	

毎 ノ	カイ	海	悔	マイ	毎	バイ	梅
R-1302		R-1303		R-1304		R-1305	
ブ	侮	ビン	敏	ハン	繁		
R-1306		R-1307		R-1308			

晦		カイ			**2452**
R-2773	晦渋	カイジュウ	obscurity; ambiguity		
	晦日	みそか	last day of the month		

| 参 | シン | 診 | チン | 珍 |
| R-1656 | | R-1940 | | |

| 疹 | | シン | | | **2574** |
| R-2774 | 麻疹 | マシン | measles | | |

滲		シン			**2291**
R-2775	滲出	シンシュツ	percolation; exuding		
	滲む	にじむ	spread; blot		
	滲る	しみる	to blot		

| 謬 | | ビュウ | | | **2720** |
| R-2776 | 無謬性 | ムビュウセイ | infallibility | | |

由 ノ	チュウ	宙	抽	ユ	由	油	ジク	軸
	R-1347		R-1348		R-1345	R-1346		R-1349
シュウ	袖	テキ	笛	ユウ	由		
R-1350		R-2147		R-1345			

| 紬 | | チュウ | | | **2666** |
| R-2777 | 紬 | つむぎ | pongee | | |

| 迪 | | テキ | | | **2412** |
| R-2778 | 啓迪 | ケイテキ | teach; guide | | |

	迪	みち	used in names

柚		ユ		2486
R-2779	柚(子)	ユズ	citron	

㞢	ショウ	裳	賞	償	掌	ジョウ	常
		R-1338	R-1339	R-1340	R-1341		R-1342
	ドウ	堂	トウ	党			
		R-1343		R-1344			

嘗		ショウ・ジョウ		2870
R-2780	大嘗祭	ダイジョウサイ	festival of thanks following enthronment of an emperor	

炎	タン	淡	エン	炎	ダン	談
⟋		R-1887		R-2029		R-994

痰		タン		2573
R-2781	血痰	ケッタン	bloody phlegm	

CHAPTER 11

A Potpourri of Readings

INTUITION FROM DOMINANT PRIMITIVE

WE BEGIN this hodge-podge of readings with a group of kanji whose *on-yomi* you should be able to guess by "intuition" from the dominant primitive, even though there are too many exceptions to allow us to make a group as such.

雉 R-2782		チ		2584
	雉(子)	きじ	pheasant	

堆 R-2783		タイ		2185
	堆積岩	タイセキガン	rocks piled up high	
	堆い	うずたかい	be piled up high	

椎 R-2784		スイ・ツイ		2505
	椎骨	ツイコツ	vertebra	
	椎	しい	chinquapin	
	椎	つち	used in names	
	椎茸	しいたけ	kind of mushroom	

錐 R-2785		スイ		2760
	錐形	スイケイ	pyramid-shaped	
	錐	きり	a gimlet; a drill	

誰 R-2786		スイ		2712
	誰何	スイカ	Who goes there?	
	誰	だれ	who	

惟 R-2787		イ・ユイ		2276
	惟惟	イイ	sound expressing assent	
	惟みる	おもんみる	consider; reflect	
	惟	これ	this (classical)	
	惟	ただ	used in names	

仇 R-2788		キュウ		2114
	仇敵	キュウテキ	bitter enemy	
	仇	あだ	enemy; enmity	

佃 R-2789		デン		2111
	佃作	デンサク	farming	
	佃	つくだ	new field	

侶 R-2790		リョ		2121
	伴侶	ハンリョ	companion; associate	

廻 R-2791		カイ		2886
	廻船	カイセン	barge; cargo vessel	
	廻る	まわる	go around	

屍 R-2792		シ		2222
	屍骸	シガイ	corpse; remains	
	屍	しかばね	corpse; remains	
	屍	かばね	corpse; remains	

洸 R-2793		コウ		2286
	洸々	コウコウ	rough; crude	

胱 R-2794		コウ		2457
	膀胱	ボウコウ	urinary bladder	

仔 R-2795		シ		2113
	仔細	シサイ	circumstances	

歎 R-2796		タン	2859
	歎異抄	タンイショウ	*Notes Lamenting Differences* (famous work by the noted Buddhist reformer, Shinran)
	歎く	なげく	grief; lamentation

箪 R-2797		タン	2631
	箪笥	タンス	cabinet

汝 R-2798		ジョ	2303
	汝	なんじ	thou

沐 R-2799		モク	2293
	沐浴	モクヨク	bathing

栖 R-2800		セイ	2497
	栖	す	nest
	栖む	すむ	roost; dwell

洒 R-2801		シャ・サイ	2292
	洒脱	シャダツ	free-thinking; unconventional
	洒掃	サイソウ	cleaning

涜 R-2802		トク	2297
	冒涜	ボウトク	blasphemy

斡 R-2803		アツ	2781
	斡旋	アッセン	good offices; services

旺 R-2804		オウ	2450
	旺盛	オウセイ	flourishing; prospering
	旺ん	さかん	flourishing; prospering
	旺	あきら	used in names

灘		タン		2321
R-2805	灘	なだ	open sea	
芯		シン		2368
R-2806	帯芯	タイシン	sash padding	
硯		ケン		2589
R-2807	唐硯	トウケン	Chinese ink slab	
	硯	すずり	inkstone	
鴻		コウ		2313
R-2808	鴻野	コウの	(family name)	
	鴻	おおとり	giant swan	
	鴻	ひろ	used in names	
馴		ジュン		2807
R-2809	馴養	ジュンヨウ	tame; domesticate	
	馴れる	なれる	get used to	
蝉		セン		2692
R-2810	蝉	せみ	cicada	
餌		ジ		2797
R-2811	食餌	ショクジ	diet	
	餌	え	bait	
	餌	えさ	animal feed	
釦		コウ		2754
R-2812	釦	ボタン	button	
釜		フ		2332
R-2813	釜山	フザン	Pusan (Korean city)	
	釜	かま	iron pot; kettle	

斧 R-2814		フ		2333
	石斧	セキフ	stone axe	
	斧	おの	axe	

杓 R-2815		シャク		2510
	杓子	シャクシ	dipper; ladle	

灼 R-2816		シャク		2544
	灼熱	シャクネツ	incandescent heat	
	灼く	やく	to burn	

鵡 R-2817		ム		2831
	鸚鵡	オウム	parrot	

楢 R-2818		ユウ		2493
	楢	なら	Japanese oak	

頌 R-2819		ショウ		2794
	頌歌	ショウカ	song of praise	
	頌える	たたえる	sing the praises of	
	頌める	ほめる	to praise	

INTUITION FROM MEANING

The *on-yomi* for this next group of kanji can be guessed at from their meaning. That is, the reading of another, more common character of the same meaning supplies the reading. To help you, the character of related meaning is given in each frame.

泪 R-2820	→ 涙	ルイ		2294
	泪	なみだ	tear	

碧 R-2821	→ 壁	ヘキ		2588
	碧巌禄	ヘキガンロク	*Blue Cliff Records* (classic Zen kōan collection)	
	碧	あお	used in names	
	碧	みどり	used in names	

蕊 R-2822	→ 髄	ズイ		2393
	雌蕊	シズイ	pistil	

聯 R-2823	→ 連	レン		2676
	聯隊	レンタイ	regiment	

惣 R-2824	→ 総	ソウ		2432
	惣菜	ソウザイ	side dish	

綜 R-2825	→ 総	ソウ		2660
	綜合	ソウゴウ	comprehensive; synthetic	
	綜べる	すべる	to rule; control	
	綜	おさ	used in names	

潰 R-2826	→ 壊	カイ		2319
	潰滅	カイメツ	destruction; demolition	
	潰れる	つぶれる	destroy	

尖 R-2827	→ 先	セン		2903
	尖頭	セントウ	pinnacle; spire; steeple	
	尖る	とがる	come to a point	

焔 R-2828	→ 炎	エン		2546
	火焔	カエン	fire; blaze	
	焔	ほのお	flames	
	焔	ほむら	flames	

蒐 R-2829	→ 集・輯	シュウ		2409
	蒐集家	シュウシュウカ	collector	

彊 R-2830	→ 強	キョウ		2240
	自彊	ジキョウ	strenuous effort	
彬 R-2831	→ 賓	ヒン		2529
	彬々	ビンビン	splendid form	
	彬	あき	used in names	
	彬	あきら	used in names	
	彬	あや	used in names	
恢 R-2832	→ 快・回	カイ		2282
	恢復	カイフク	recovery	
晋 R-2833	→ 進	シン		2436
	晋む	すすむ	to advance	
	晋	あき	used in names	
	晋	くに	used in names	
	晋	ゆき	used in names	
翰 R-2834	→ 簡	カン		2780
	翰墨	カンボク	writing brush and ink	
	翰	やまどり	copper pheasant	
籤 R-2835	→ 選	セン		2082
	籤	くじ	drawing of lots	
	籤	かずとり	tally	
疏 R-2836	→ 書	ソ・ショ		2922
	諫疏	カンソ	written advice to the throne	
	疏い	うとい	distant; alienated	

UNCLASSIFIED READINGS

The *on yomi* for this next group can be guessed at from their meaning. That is, the reading of another, more common character of the same meaning supplies the reading. To help you, the character will often be supplied in the frame.

於 R-2837		オ		2900
	於いて	おいて	in; at	
	於	ああ	Ah! (exclamation)	
	於	うえ	used in names	
	於	お	used in names	
	The reading of this character was learned in VOL. 2 as the root character for the *hiragana* お.			

蝕 R-2838		ショク		2800
	月蝕	ゲッショク	lunar eclipse	
	蝕む	むしばむ	be worm eaten	

兎 R-2839		ト		2093
	兎に角	トにカク	anyhow; in any case	
	兎	うさぎ	rabbit	

醍 R-2840		ダイ		2747
	醍醐味	ダイゴミ	zest for life	

宥 R-2841		ユウ		2210
	宥恕	ユウジョ	indulgence; pardon	
	宥める	なだめる	soothe; pacify	
	宥す	ゆるす	forgive	
	宥	すけ	used in names	
	宥	みろ	used in names	

勾 R-2842		コウ		2148
	勾配	コウバイ	slope; gradient	

禽 R-2843		キン		2049
	禽獣	キンジュウ	birds and beasts	
	禽	とり	bird	

檎 R-2844		ゴ・キン		2050
	林檎	リンゴ	apple	

罵 R-2845		バ		2699
	罵倒	バトウ	denunciation; abuse	
	罵る	ののしる	verbally abuse	

櫓 R-2846		ロ		2508
	櫓櫂	ロカイ	oars	
	櫓	やぐら	turret; tower	

竺 R-2847		ジク		2642
	天竺	テンジク	India; a foreign land	

云 R-2848		ウン		2102
	云々	ウンウン・ウンヌン	etc., etc.	

匙 R-2849		シ・ヒ		2891
	匙	さじ	spoon	

淫 R-2850		イン		2298
	淫乱	インラン	debauchery; lewdness	

絨 R-2851		ジュウ		2657
	絨毯	ジュウタン	carpet	

脩 R-2852		シュウ		2130
	脩める	おさめる	cultivate; pursue	
	脩	おさむ	used in names	

紗		サ・シャ		2673
R-2853	薄紗	ハクサ	gauze; gossamer	
	紗	うすぎぬ	light silk	

欣		キン		2888
R-2854	欣々然	キンキンゼン	joyfully	
	欣	やすし	used in names	
	欣	よし	used in names	

芹		キン		2396
R-2855	芹	せり	parsley	

燦		サン		2543
R-2856	燦然	サンゼン	brilliance; radiance	
	燦らか	あきらか	clear	

爽		ソウ		2855
R-2857	爽快	ソウカイ	refreshing	
	爽やか	さわやか	refreshing; bracing	
	爽	さや	used in names	

雀		ジャク		2878
R-2858	孔雀	クジャク	peacock; peahen	
	雀	すずめ	sparrow	

豹		ヒョウ		2734
R-2859	豹変	ヒョウヘン	sudden change	

衿		キン		2623
R-2860	開衿	カイキン	open collar	
	衿	えり	collar	

沃		ヨク		2079
R-2861	沃地	ヨクチ	fertile land	

妖 R-2862		ヨウ		2078
	妖女	ヨウジョ	fairy	
	妖しい	あやしい	dubious; fishy	

濾 R-2863		ロ		2328
	濾過	ロカ	filtering	

怯 R-2864		キョウ		2275
	怯れる	おそれる	to fear	

劫 R-2865		ゴウ		2857
	劫火	ゴウカ	world-destroying fire	

厨 R-2866		ズ・チュウ		2152
	厨子	ズシ	miniature shrine	
	厨房	チュウボウ	kitchen; galley	

赳 R-2867		キュウ		2936
	赳	たけ	used in names	
	赳	たけし	used in names	

篭 R-2868		ロウ		2638
	印篭	インロウ	pillbox	
	篭める	こめる	to load; fill up	
	篭	かご	cage	

聾 R-2869		ロウ		2983
	聾学校	ロウガッコウ	school for the deaf	

胚 R-2870		ハイ		2458
	胚芽	ハイガ	germ; embryo bud	

芦 R-2871		ロ	2364
	芦汀	ロテイ	shoreline with reeds
	芦	あし	reed

桶 R-2872		トウ	2530
	桶	おけ	bucket

茸 R-2873		ジョウ	2394
	茸	たけ	mushroom

繋 R-2874		ケイ	2655
	繋留	ケイリュウ	mooring
	繋ぐ	つなぐ	fasten; tie

柊 R-2875		シュウ	2485
	柊	ひいらぎ	holly tree

吃 R-2876		キツ	2175
	吃音	キツオン	stammering
	吃る	どもる	stammer; stutter

貼 R-2877		チョウ・テン	2736
	貼用	チョウヨウ	pasting; affixing
	貼附	テンプ	pasting; affixing
	貼る	はる	to stick; paste

帖 R-2878		チョウ	2231
	法帖	ホウチョウ	copy book printed from old calligraphy masters' works
	帖	チョウ	notebook

捷 R-2879		ショウ	2273
	捷径	ショウケイ	short cut
	捷い	はやい	fast

	捷	さとし	used in names	
	捷	とし	used in names	
	捷	まさる	used in names	
	捷	かつ	used in names	
鮎		デン		2817
R-2880	鮎	あゆ	sweet smelt	
嚢		ノウ		2883
R-2881	胆嚢	タンノウ	gallbladder	
	嚢	ふくろ	pouch; bag	
叢		ソウ		2895
R-2882	叢書	ソウショ	anthology; collection	
	叢	くさむら	clump of bushes; thicket	
鍾		ショウ		2772
R-2883	鍾乳石	ショウニュウセキ	stalactites	
	鍾まる	あつまる	gather together	
腫		シュ		2467
R-2884	腫脹	シュチョウ	swelling; boil	
	腫れる	はれる	become swollen	
孜		シ		2209
R-2885	孜々	シシ	assiduously	
	孜める	つとめる	work diligently	
駁		バク		2808
R-2886	反駁	ハンバク	refutation	
卿		ケイ・キョウ		2898
R-2887	卿等	ケイラ	high court officials	
	枢機卿	スウキキョウ	cardinal (Catholic)	

腔		コウ		2465
R-2888	口腔	コウコウ	oral (medicine)	
	腔	から	empty; hollow	
	腔	からだ	body	
牟		ム・ボウ		2961
R-2889	釈迦牟尼	シャカムニ	Shakyamuni the Buddha	
	牟ぼる	むさぼる	covet; greed for	
眸		ボウ		2580
R-2890	双眸	ソウボウ	one's eyes	
	眸	ひとみ	pupil of the eye	
彗		スイ		2850
R-2891	彗星	スイセイ	comet	
	彗	ほうき	comet	
	彗	さとし	used in names	
弥		ビ・ミ		2241
R-2892	弥縫	ビホウ	stopgap; temporizing	
	弥撒	ミサ	Catholic mass	
	弥	いや	all the more; increasingly	
	弥	や	used in names	
	弥	わたる	used in names	
	弥	ひさ	used in names	
	弥	ひろ	used in names	
	弥	ます	used in names	
	弥	みつ	used in names	
慧		エ・ケイ		2851
R-2893	慧業	エゴウ	practicing Buddhist discipline	
	慧眼	ケイガン	keen eye	
祢		ネ		2601
R-2894	祢宜	ネギ	ritual Shinto priest	

股 R-2895		コ	2454
	股肱	ココウ	second self; right-hand helper
	股	また	crotch; groin
	股	もも	thigh; femur

菩 R-2896		ボ	2957
	菩提	ボダイ	enlightenment (*bodhi*)

歪 R-2897		ワイ	2862
	歪曲	ワイキョク	distortion; falsification
	歪む	ゆがむ	warp; get distorted

焚 R-2898		フン	2537
	焚書抗儒	フンショコウジュ	burning Chinese classics and burying Confucian scholars alive
	焚く	たく	kindle; build a fire
	焚く	やく	to burn

毅 R-2899		キ	2889
	毅然	キゼン	dauntless; resolute
	毅	つよし	used in names
	毅	かた	used in names
	毅	たけし	used in names
	毅	さだむ	used in names
	毅	たか	used in names
	毅	たけ	used in names
	毅	とし	used in names

梁 R-2900		リョウ	2299
	棟梁	トウリョウ	pillar; chief support
	梁	はり	beam; girder

酎 R-2901		チュウ	2748
	焼酎	ショウチュウ	low-class saké

妬		ト	2195
R-2902	嫉妬	シット	jealousy; envy
	妬む	ねたむ	be jealous; envy
	妬く	やく	burn with jealousy

粟		ゾク	2654
R-2903	粟粒	ゾクリュウ	millet seeds

妾		ショウ	2622
R-2904	妾腹	ショウフク	child by a concubine
	妾	めかけ	concubine; mistress

珊		サン	2561
R-2905	珊瑚	サンゴ	coral

琢		タク	2560
R-2906	琢磨	タクマ	diligent application
	琢	あや	used in names
	琢	たか	used in names

亮		リョウ	2920
R-2907	亮	あきら	used in names
	亮	あき	used in names
	亮	すけ	used in names
	亮	かつ	used in names
	亮	まこと	used in names
	亮	ふさ	used in names
	亮	たすく	used in names

鄭		テイ	2425
R-2908	鄭重	テイチョウ	courtesy; civility

牽		ケン	2550
R-2909	牽制	ケンセイ	check; restraint

捺 R-2910		ナツ		2250
	捺印	ナツイン	affixing a seal to	
	捺す	おす	press down	
	捺	とし	used in names	

套 R-2911		トウ		2901
	常套	ジョウトウ	conventional	

剥 R-2912		ハク		2145
	剥製術	ハクセイジュツ	taxidermy	
	剥ぐ	はぐ	to peel off	

眉 R-2913		ビ		2583
	柳眉	リュウビ	crescent eyebrows	
	眉	まゆ	eyebrows	

呑 R-2914		ドン		2080
	併呑	ヘイドン	annexation; absorption	
	呑む	のむ	to drink	

脊 R-2915		セキ		2071
	脊髄	セキズイ	spinal cord	

耽 R-2916		タン		2679
	耽美主義	タンビシュギ	aestheticism	

繍 R-2917		シュウ		2665
	刺繍	シシュウ	embroidery	
	繍	ぬいとり	crewelwork	

綴 R-2918		テイ		2073
	点綴	テンテイ	interspersion	
	綴じる	とじる	bind; stitch	
	綴る	つづる	to spell (words)	

螺		ラ		2691
R-2919	螺旋形	ラセンケイ	spiral-shaped; helical	
柵		サク		2507
R-2920	柵	とりで	fortress	
	柵	しがらみ	weir	
杵		ショ		2503
R-2921	杵	きね	pestle	
寵		チョウ		2982
R-2922	恩寵	オンチョウ	grace; divine favor	
叩		コウ		2166
R-2923	叩頭	コウトウ	kowtow	
	叩く	たたく	to beat on	
叱		シツ		2179
R-2924	叱責	シッセキ	reproof; reproach	
	叱る	しかる	to scold	
宋		ソウ		2215
R-2925	宋朝	ソウチョウ	Sung dynasty	
塞		ソク・サイ		2214
R-2926	閉塞	ヘイソク	blockade	
	防塞	ボウサイ	barricade	
	塞ぐ	ふさぐ	to block up	
	塞	とりで	fortress	
牢		ロウ		2213
R-2927	牢屋	ロウや	prison; jail	
	牢	ひとや	prison	

姦		カン		2194
R-2928	姦通	カンツウ	adultery	
	姦しい	かしましい	boisterous	

啄		タク		2168
R-2929	啄む	ついばむ	to peck at	
	啄く	たたく	to beat on	

呪		ジュ		2169
R-2930	呪文	ジュモン	curse; spell	
	呪う	のろう	to curse	

吠		バイ		2170
R-2931	吠える	ほえる	to bark	

叡		エイ		2905
R-2932	叡智	エイチ	wisdom; intellect	
	叡らか	あきらか	clear	
	叡	あきら	used in names	
	叡	さとし	used in names	
	叡	ただ	used in names	
	叡	とおる	used in names	
	叡	とし	used in names	
	叡	まさ	used in names	

厭		エン		2149
R-2933	厭世	エンセイ	pessimism; world-weariness	
	厭きる	あきる	be fed up	
	厭う	いとう	loathe	

鳳		ホウ		2142
R-2934	鳳仙花	ホウセンカ	balsam; touch-me-not	
	鳳	おおとり	great swan	
	鳳	たか	used in names	

昂 R-2935		コウ		2449
	昂然	コウゼン	elated; triumphant	
	昂	たかし	used in names	
	昂	あきら	used in names	
	昂	たか	used in names	

欝 R-2936		ウツ		2856
	憂欝	ユウウツ	melancholy; depression	

壷 R-2937		コ		2904
	銅壷	ドウコ	copper boiler	
	壷	つぼ	pot	

酋 R-2938		シュウ		2906
	酋長	シュウチョウ	chief; chieftain	
	酋	おさ	chief; head	
	酋	かしら	head	

燭 R-2939		ショク・ソク		2539
	燭光	ショッコウ	candlepower	
	蝋燭	ロウソク	candle	
	燭	ともしび	torch	

溺 R-2940		デキ		2308
	溺愛	デキアイ	dotage; infatuation	
	溺れる	おぼれる	to sink; drown	

浩 R-2941		コウ		2311
	浩然	コウゼン	expansive; broadminded	
	浩	ひろし	used in names	
	浩	ひろ	used in names	
	浩	ゆたか	used in names	

櫛		シツ		2476
R-2942	櫛比	シッピ	lined up close together	
	櫛	くし	comb	

蝋		ロウ		2688
R-2943	蝋燭	ロウソク	candle	

穿		セン		2616
R-2944	穿孔機	センコウキ	drill press	
	穿つ	うがつ	to bore; drill	

碍		ガイ		2592
R-2945	碍子	ガイシ	insulator	
	碍げる	さまたげる	to obstruct	

夙		シュク		2141
R-2946	夙に	つとに	early in the morning	
	夙い	はやい	early	

牝		ヒン		2551
R-2947	牝馬	ヒンバ	a mare	
	牝	めす	female	

牡		ボ		2552
R-2948	牡丹	ボタン	tree peony	
	牡	おす	male	

癌		ガン		2576
R-2949	肺癌	ハイガン	lung cancer	

蛋		タン		2683
R-2950	蛋白質	タンパクシツ	protein	

弄		ロウ		2558
R-2951	侮弄	ブロウ	ridicule	
	弄ぶ	もてあそぶ	to toy with	
渕		エン		2325
R-2952	渕底	エンテイ	bottom of the abyss	
	渕	ふち	deep pool	
溢		イツ		2315
R-2953	溢血	イッケツ	internal hemorrhage	
	溢れる	あふれる	to overflow	
萌		ホウ		2377
R-2954	萌芽	ホウガ	germination; sprout	
	萌す	きざす	show signs of	
	萌	めばえ	bud	
	萌える	もえる	burst into bloom	
	萌	もえ	used in names	
	萌	あ	used in names	
萄		ドウ		2379
R-2955	葡萄	ブドウ	grapes	
罫		ケイ		2698
R-2956	罫紙	ケイシ	lined paper	
錫		シャク		2764
R-2957	錫杖	シャクジョウ	a priest's staff	
	錫	すず	tin	
塵		ジン		2838
R-2958	塵芥	ジンカイ	dust; garbage	
	塵	ちり	dust	

稽 R-2959		ケイ		2088
	稽古	ケイコ	practice; training	
	稽える	かんがえる	to ponder	
橘 R-2960		キツ		2494
	柑橘類	カンキツルイ	citrus fruits	
	橘	たちばな	mandarin orange	
戚 R-2961		セキ		2882
	親戚	シンセキ	relatives	
蘇 R-2962		ソ		2380
	蘇生	ソセイ	revival; resurrection	
鼎 R-2963		テイ		2865
	鼎談	テイダン	tripartite talks	
	鼎	かなえ	tripod	
鼠 R-2964		ソ		2065
	鼠	ねずみ	rat	
禿 R-2965		トク		2606
	禿頭	トクトウ	baldness; bald head	
	禿	はげ	bald	
	禿	かむろ	short hair of a child	
薮 R-2966		ソウ		2403
	薮	やぶ	thicket	
吻 R-2967		フン		2174
	接吻	セップン	kiss	

嬰 R-2968			エイ	2193
	嬰児	エイジ	infant	
侃 R-2969			カン	2123
	侃々諤々	カンカンガクガク	outspoken	
	侃い	つよい	strong and proper	
	侃	あきら	used in names	
	侃	ただし	used in names	
	侃	なお	used in names	
	侃	やす	used in names	
撒 R-2970			サツ・サン	2271
	撒水	サンスイ	watering; sprinkling	
	撒く	まく	to scatter	
叉 R-2971			サ・シャ	2914
	音叉	オンサ	tuning fork	
	夜叉	ヤシャ	she-devil	
	叉	また	fork; crotch	
轟 R-2972			ゴウ	2729
	轟音	ゴウオン	deafening roar	
	轟く	とどろく	to roar; rumble	
臼 R-2973			キュウ	2063
	脱臼	ダッキュウ	dislocation	
	臼	うす	mortar	
臥 R-2974			ガ	2909
	行住臥座	ギョウジュウガザ	the 4 cardinal Buddhist activities: walking, stopping, sitting, lying	
	臥す	ふす	lie prostrate	

腎		ジン		2453
R-2975	腎臓	ジンゾウ	kidney	

薩		サツ		2956
R-2976	薩摩薯	サツマいも	sweet potato	

悶		モン		2775
R-2977	悶絶	モンゼツ	faint; fall in convulsions	
	悶える	もだえる	be in agony	

隙		ゲキ		2426
R-2978	間隙	カンゲキ	gap; opening; crevice	
	隙	すき	chink; crack	
	隙	ひま	chink; time	

讐		シュウ		2707
R-2979	復讐	フクシュウ	revenge	
	讐	あだ	foe	

肘		チュウ		2464
R-2980	肘	ひじ	elbow	

肋		ロク		2463
R-2981	肋骨	ロッコツ	ribs	
	肋	あばら	ribs	

蔑		ベツ		2390
R-2982	軽蔑	ケイベツ	derision	
	蔑む	さげすむ	to deride	

燕		エン		2869
R-2983	燕尾服	エンビフク	swallow-tailed coat	
	燕	つばめ	swallow	

蓋 R-2984		ガイ		2388
	天蓋	テンガイ	canopy	
	蓋	ふた	lid	
	蓋う	おおう	to cover	

閃 R-2985		セン		2774
	閃光	センコウ	flash of light	
	閃く	ひらめく	to flash; fulgurate	

糞 R-2986		フン		2653
	糞便	フンベン	excrement	
	糞	くそ	dung	

拭 R-2987		ショク		2254
	払拭	フッショク	sweep away; wipe out	
	拭う	ぬぐう	wipe off	
	拭く	ふく	wipe	

屢 R-2988		ル		2221
	屢次	ルジ	in succession	
	屢	しばしば	frequently	

胤 R-2989		イン		2921
	後胤	コウイン	descendant	
	胤	たね	issue; offspring	
	胤	かず	used in names	
	胤	つぎ	used in names	
	胤	つぐ	used in names	

夷 R-2990		イ		2881
	東夷	トウイ	eastern barbarians	
	夷	えびす	barbarian	

鹵		ロ		2866
R-2991	鹵獲	ロカク	capture	
	鹵	しお	rock salt	

茜		セン		2407
R-2992	茜	あかね	madder; red dye	

烹		ホウ		2549
R-2993	割烹	カッポウ	cooking	

茅		ボウ		2385
R-2994	茅屋	ボウオク	thatched cottage	
	茅	かや	miscanthus reed	
	茅	ち	used in names	

擢		テキ		2272
R-2995	抜擢	バッテキ	select; choose	
	擢んでる	ぬきんでる	excel; surpass	

捗		チョク		2269
R-2996	進捗	シンチョク	progress; advance	
	捗る	はかどる	to progress	

那		ナ		2960
R-2997	旦那	ダンナ	master; husband	
	那	とも	used in names	

駄		ダ		2804
R-2998	飛騨	ヒダ	area in Gifu Prefecture	

穎		エイ		2790
R-2999	穎脱	エイダツ	gain recognition	

鶯 R-3000		オウ		2907
	鶯	うぐいす	Japanese bush warbler	

尤 R-3001		ユウ		2087
	尤物	ユウブツ	something superior	
	尤も	もっとも	reasonable; of course	

貌 R-3002		ボウ		2733
	全貌	ゼンボウ	overview; full picture	

匡 R-3003		キョウ		2892
	匡	たすく	used in names	
	匡	まさ	used in names	
	匡	ただし	used in names	

穆 R-3004		ボク		2612
	穆々	ボクボク	quiet; dutiful	

肇 R-3005		チョウ		2893
	肇	はじめ	used in names	
	肇	とし	used in names	
	肇	はつ	used in names	

樗 R-3006		チョ		2526
	樗蒲一	チョボイチ	game played with one die	

皐 R-3007		コウ		2070
	皐	さつき	5th lunar month; rainy season	

郁 R-3008		イク		2424
	郁	あや	used in names	
	郁	か	used in names	
	郁	かおり	used in names	
	郁	かおる	used in names	
	郁	ふみ	used in names	

杜 R-3009		ト		2500
	杜氏	トジ・トウジ	saké maker	
	杜	もり	woods	
	杜る	とじる	to close	

纏 R-3010		テン		2663
	纏綿	テンメン	involvement; entanglement	
	纏わる	まつわる	coil around; follow about	
	纏う	まとう	attire oneself	

蒙 R-3011		モウ		2384
	啓蒙主義	ケイモウシュギ	Enlightenment (European)	
	蒙る	こうむる	be subjected to; suffer loss	

餐 R-3012		サン		2798
	粗餐	ソサン	plain meal	

肴 R-3013		コウ		2896
	酒肴	シュコウ	food and drink	
	肴	さかな	tidbits; relish	

碩 R-3014		セキ		2593
	碩学	セキガク	erudite scholar	
	碩	みち	used in names	
	碩	みつる	used in names	
	碩	ひろ	used in names	

拶 R-3015		サツ		2261
	挨拶	アイサツ	greetings; salutations	

斯 R-3016		シ		2890
	斯界	シカイ	this world; this field	
	斯	この	this	

湛		タン・チン		2317
R-3017	湛然	タンゼン	overflowing	
	湛える	たたえる	fill up	

犀		サイ・セイ		2069
R-3018	犀	サイ	rhinoceros	
	木犀	モクセイ	devilwood tree	

巾		キン		2101
R-3019	布巾	フキン	rag; cloth	
	巾	はば	width; breadth; range	

姪		テツ		2201
R-3020	姪孫	テッソン	grandniece	
	姪	めい	niece	

枕		チン		2472
R-3021	枕席	チンセキ	pillow and bed	
	枕	まくら	pillow	

倶		ク		2124
R-3022	倶楽部	クラブ	club	

諺		ゲン		2723
R-3023	俗諺	ゾクゲン	common saying	
	諺	ことわざ	maxim; proverb	

喧		ケン		2163
R-3024	喧嘩	ケンカ	a quarrel	
	喧しい	かまびすしい	noisy	
	喧しい	やかましい	noisy	

掴		カク		2249
R-3025	掴む	つかむ	grab; grasp	
	掴み	つかみ	a handful	

魁		カイ		2924
R-3026	首魁	シュカイ	ringleader	
	魁	さきがけ	vanguard	
	魁	かしら	chief; leader	
	魁	いさお	used in names	
	魁	いさむ	used in names	
	魁	つとむ	used in names	

輿		ヨ		2860
R-3027	輿論	ヨロン	public opinion	
	輿	こし	palanquin; bier	

柘		シャ		2517
R-3028	柘	つげ	box tree	

已		イ		2937
R-3029	已に	すでに	already; yet	
	已む	やむ	stop; quit	

蟄		チツ		2684
R-3030	蟄居	チッキョ	staying indoors	

祀		シ		2992
R-3031	祭祀	サイシ	religious service	
	祀る	まつる	worship; enshrine	

祓		フツ		2993
R-3032	修祓	シュウフツ	Shinto purification	
	祓う	はらう	purify; exorcise	

棘		キョク		2938
R-3033	荊棘	ケイキョク	thorns; brambles	
	棘	とげ	thorns	

躓		チ		2740
R-3034	顚躓	テンチ	fall head-over-heels	
	躓く	つまずく	stumble	

厖		ボウ		2089
R-3035	厖大	ボウダイ	enormous	
	厖きい	おおきい	large	

咎		キュウ		2156
R-3036	咎戒	キュウカイ	admonition; a warning	
	咎める	とがめる	rebuke; criticize; challenge	
	咎	とが	fault; blame	

站		タン		2620
R-3037	兵站	ヘイタン	impedimenta	
	站つ	たつ	come to a stop	

聚		ジュウ・ジュ		2939
R-3038	聚落	シュウラク	colony	
	聚まる	あつまる	gather	

鑿		サク		2066
R-3039	穿鑿	センサク	sorting; delving into	
	鑿	のみ	chisel	

巫		フ		2930
R-3040	巫術	フジュツ	shamanism	
	巫	みこ	Shinto priestess	

憑 R-3041		ヒョウ		2428
	憑依	ヒョウイ	possession (by a spirit)	
	憑かれる	つかれる	be possessed	
	憑く	つく	obsess; possess	
刹 R-3042		サツ・セツ		2144
	名刹	メイサツ	famous temple	
	刹那	セツナ	an instant; a moment	
毀 R-3043		キ		2067
	毀損	キソン	damage; injury	
	毀れる	こぼれる	be broken	
梟 R-3044		キョウ		2837
	梟首	キョウシュ	decapitation	
	梟	ふくろう	an owl	
凛 R-3045		リン		2138
	凛々	リンリン	intense	
	凛しい	きびしい	severe	
	凛い	さむい	cold	
昴 R-3046		ボウ		2435
	昴	すばる	the Pleiades	
懺 R-3047		サン・ザン		2083
	懺悔	サンゲ・ザンゲ	confession; repentance	
翔 R-3048		ショウ		2933
	翔破	ショウハ	fly; cover	
	翔る	かける	fly; soar	
漱 R-3049		ソウ		2288
	夏目漱石	なつめソウセキ	Natsume Sōseki (novelist)	

	漱く	くちそそぐ	rinse one's mouth	
	漱ぐ	すすぐ	rinse out	
翠		スイ		2863
R-3050	翠	みどり	used in names	
倅		サイ		2131
R-3051	倅	せがれ	one's own son	
呆		ボウ・ホウ		2181
R-3052	呆然	ボウゼン	amazement	
	阿呆	アホ	idiot; fool	
	呆れる	あきれる	be astonished	
躊		チュウ		2996
R-3053	躊躇	チュウチョ	vacillation; hesitation	
祷		トウ		2598
R-3054	祈祷	キトウ	prayer	
	祷る	いのる	to pray	
仄		ソク		2153
R-3055	仄聞	ソクブン	learn by hearsay	
	仄か	ほのか	faint; indistinct	
吊		チョウ		2171
R-3056	吊り	つり	hanging strap	
	吊る	つる	to hang; suspend	
叶		キョウ		2173
R-3057	叶う	かなう	be able; be realized	
	叶う	かのう	used in names	
	叶	やす	used in names	

邑 R-3058		ユウ		2180
	邑人	ユウジン	townsfolk	
	邑	むら	town	
	邑	くに	used in names	
	邑	さとし	used in names	
	邑	すみ	used in names	

庄 R-3059		ショウ		2238
	庄屋	ショウヤ	squire	
	庄	たいら	used in names	
	庄	まさ	used in names	

挨 R-3060		アイ		2248
	挨拶	アイサツ	greetings; salutations	

涅 R-3061		ネ		2331
	涅槃	ネハン	nirvana	

葱 R-3062		ソウ		2389
	葱	ねぎ	onion	

葵 R-3063		キ		2391
	葵	あおい	hollyhock; mallow	
	葵	まもる	used for names	

這 R-3064		シャ		2414
	這般	シャハン	such; of this kind	
	這う	はう	to crawl	

橇 R-3065		セイ・ゼイ・キョウ		2521
	橇	そり	sled	

瑞 R-3066		ズイ		2563
	瑞祥	ズイショウ	good omen	

	瑞	みず	water	
	瑞	たま	used in names	

		ヒツ		2570
R-3067	畢竟	ヒッキョウ	in the final analysis	
	畢に	ついに	in the end	
	畢わる	おわる	to end	

竈		ソウ		2617
R-3068	竈	かまど	furnace; oven	
	竈	かま	stove	
	竈	へっつい	hearth	

聘		ヘイ		2678
R-3069	招聘	ショウヘイ	summons; invitation	
	聘す	めす	to call; summons	

諄		ジュン		2706
R-3070	諄々	ジュンジュン	repeatedly; patiently	
	諄ろ	ねんごろ	polite	
	諄	あつし	used in names	
	諄	とも	used in names	
	諄	まこと	used in names	

諏		ス・シュ		2722
R-3071	諏訪	スワ	area in Nagano Prefecture	
	諏る	はかる	to confer; consult	

駈		ク		2809
R-3072	駈ける	かける	to set off	

驢		ロ		2810
R-3073	驢馬	ロバ	donkey	

鳶 R-3074	鳶	エン / と(ん)び	black kite	2836
鰭 R-3075	鰭	キ / ひれ	fin	2827
鸚 R-3076	鸚鵡	オウ・ヨウ / オウム	parrot	2830
鴨 R-3077	鴨	オウ / かも	duck	2835
兜 R-3078	兜	ト・トウ / かぶと	helmet	2854
勃 R-3079	勃起 / 勃る	ボツ / ボッキ / おこる	erection / to occur; arise	2858
彪 R-3080	彪 / 彪 / 彪 / 彪	ヒョウ / あきら / あや / たけし / つよし	used in names / used in names / used in names / used in names	2876
丼 R-3081	丼	セイ / どんぶり	rice bowl	2884
拳 R-3082	拳銃 / 拳 / 拳 / 拳	ケン / ケンジュウ / こぶし / たかし / つとむ	hand gun / fist / used in names / used in names	2917

黎		レイ		2935
R-3083	黎明	レイメイ	dawn	
	黎い	おおい	a covering	
	黎い	たみ	used in names	

彙		イ		2997
R-3084	語彙	ゴイ	glossary	
	彙	はりねずみ	hedgehog	
	彙める	あつめる	to gather together	

舅		キュウ		2064
R-3085	舅	しゅうと	father-in-law	

黍		ショ		2665
R-3086	黍	きび	(Chinese) millet	

李		リ		2511
R-3087	李下	リカ	under a plum; conspicuous	
	李	すもも	Japanese plum	

鼈		ベツ		3000
R-3088	鼈甲	ベッコウ	turtle shell	
	鼈	すっぽん	snapping turtle	

CHAPTER 12

Kanji with Japanese Readings Only

IN THIS CHAPTER we will bring together all the characters learned in this volume that do not have an assigned *on-yomi* or whose *on-yomi* are too rare to bother with.

In general the readings are given in *hiragana*, although this does not necessary mean that there is a direct correspondence to a *kun-yomi*. In cases where the pronunciation is clearly based on a foreign word or an original Chinese reading, however, the reading is given in *katakana*.

姥				2204
R-3089	姥	うば	aged woman	
飴				2801
R-3090	飴	あめ	candy; rice jelly	
袷				2625
R-3091	袷	あわせ	lined kimono	
箸				2640
R-3092	箸	はし	chopsticks	
樫				2509
R-3093	樫	かし	oak	
秤				2604
R-3094	秤	はかり	balances; scales	
謎				2709
R-3095	謎	なぞ	riddle; hint	

樋				2520
R-3096	樋	ひ	gutter; downspout; aqueduct	
	樋	とい	gutter; downspout; aqueduct	

鞄				2785
R-3097	鞄	かばん	suitcase; briefcase	

樫				2491
R-3098	樫	かし	oak	

鰯				2813
R-3099	鰯	いわし	sardine	

籾				2651
R-3100	籾	もみ	unhulled rice	

粁				2946
R-3101	粁	キロメートル	kilometer	

鋲				2763
R-3102	鋲	びょう	rivet; tack; thumbnail	

匂				2147
R-3103	匂う	におう	to smell something	
	匂い	におい	a smell; a stink	

凪				2140
R-3104	凪	なぎ	a lull; a calm	
	凪ぐ	なぐ	become calm; die down	

凧				2139
R-3105	凧	たこ	kite	

榊				2490
R-3106	榊	さかき	sacred Shinto tree	

柾				2489
R-3107	柾	まさき	spindle tree	

糎				2947
R-3108	糎	センチメートル	centimeter	

栂				2488
R-3109	栂	つが	hemlock; hemlock spruce	
	栂	とが	hemlock; hemlock spruce	

椙				2528
R-3110	椙	すぎ	Japanese cedar	

宍				2216
R-3111	宍	しし	meat	

轡				2965
R-3112	轡	くつわ	horse's bit	

粥				2243
R-3113	粥	かゆ	rice gruel	

辿				2413
R-3114	辿る	たどる	pursue a course	

鯵				2818
R-3115	鯵	あじ	horse mackerel	

麿				2894
R-3116	麿	まろ	used in personal names	

蒜				2404
R-3117	蒜	ひる	garlic	
	大蒜	にんにく	garlic	

蠅				2685
R-3118	蠅	はえ	fly	

姐				2206
R-3119	姐	あね	older sister	
	姐	ねえさん	Miss	

梶				2502
R-3120	梶	かじ	oar; shaft	

蛤				2695
R-3121	蛤	はまぐり	clam	

藁				2400
R-3122	藁	わら	straw	

縞				2671
R-3123	縞	しま	stripe	

貰				2737
R-3124	貰う	もらう	get; receive; accept	
	貰	もらい	tip; gratuity	

苫				2397
R-3125	苫	とま	rush matting	

瀞				2323
R-3126	瀞	とろ	pool (in a river)	

鰹				2822
R-3127	鰹	かつお	bonito	

晒				2444
R-3128	晒す	さらす	bleach; refine; air (out)	
	晒	さらし	bleaching; bleached cotton	

鮫				2821
R-3129	鮫	さめ	shark	

榎				2514
R-3130	榎	えのき	hackberry; lotus tree	

苅				2387
R-3131	苅る	かる	mow (grass)	

鱈				2819
R-3132	鱈	たら	codfish	

鮪				2816
R-3133	鮪	まぐろ	tunny; tuna	

鮒				2825
R-3134	鮒	ふな	carp	

囁				2157
R-3135	囁く	ささやく	to whisper	

孕				2208
R-3136	孕む	はらむ	to conceive; get pregnant	

做				2132
R-3137	做す	なす	to cause to happen	

苺				2350
R-3138	苺	いちご	strawberry	

廿				2868
R-3139	廿	ニジュウ	twenty	

髭				2047
R-3140	髭	ひげ	beard; moustache	

畷				2072
R-3141	畷	なわて	path between rice paddies	

韮				2081
R-3142	韮	にら	garlic chives	

或				2091
R-3143	或る	ある	some one; a particular	

疋				2098
R-3144	疋	ひき	counter for animals	

侭				2125
R-3145	侭	まま	as is; as one likes	

俣				2127
R-3146	俣	また	crotch; thigh; fork in a road	

噂				2161
R-3147	噂	うわさ	rumor; gossip	

噛				2172
R-3148	噛む	かむ	to chew; to bite	

噺 R-3149	噺	はなし	talk; story; tale	2176
喰 R-3150	喰う 喰らう	くう くらう	eat; drink; receive a blow eat; drink; receive a blow	2182
尻 R-3151	尻	しり	buttocks; hips	2220
幡 R-3152	幡	はた	pennant; banner	2232
捌 R-3153	捌き 捌く	さばき さばく	dealing; selling to handle; deal with	2256
摺 R-3154	摺る	する	make a rubbing; imprint	2258
淀 R-3155	淀 淀む	よど よどむ	pool (in a river); backwater stagnate	2330
莨 R-3156	莨	たばこ	tobacco	2347
薙 R-3157	薙ぐ	なぐ	mow down	2353
蓑 R-3158	蓑	みの	straw raincoat	2354

蕨 R-3159				2405
	蕨	わらび	bracken; fernbrake	

迄 R-3160				2421
	迄	まで	up until; by	

桁 R-3161				2483
	桁	けた	beam; girder	

碓 R-3162				2596
	碓	うす	pedal-operated mortar	

竪 R-3163				2618
	竪	たて	vertical; upright	

篠 R-3164				2639
	篠	しの	type of small bamboo	

蛸 R-3165				2690
	蛸	たこ	octopus	

蛭 R-3166				2696
	蛭	ひる	leech	

詫 R-3167				2721
	詫び	わび	excuse; apology	
	詫びる	わびる	apologize; make an excuse	

鍋 R-3168				2757
	鍋	なべ	cooking pot; kettle	

鑓 R-3169				2767
	鑓	やり	spear; lance	

鋏				2773
R-3170	鋏	はさみ	scissors	

雫				2778
R-3171	雫	しずく	droplet; trickle	

鰍				2823
R-3172	鰍	かじか	bullhead	

鮨				2826
R-3173	鮨	すし	sushi	

鵜				2832
R-3174	鵜	う	cormorant	

覗				2875
R-3175	覗う	うかがう	spy on	
	覗き	のぞき	a peep; a glimpse	
	覗く	のぞく	to peep; to peek	

畠				2916
R-3176	畠	はたけ	field; farm	

躾				2942
R-3177	躾	しつけ	teaching manners	

祟				2945
R-3178	祟る	たたる	put a curse on; haunt	

粍				2948
R-3179	粍	ミリ	millimeter	
	粍	ミリメートル	millimeter	

吋				2952
R-3180	吋	インチ	inch	

呎				2953
R-3181	呎	フィート	foot	

鯖				2820
R-3182	鯖	さば	mackerel	

CHAPTER 13

Readings of Old and Alternate Forms

THE READINGS OF the old and alternate forms of kanji learned in chapter 6 keep the same readings as their simplified forms. For the sake of completeness, all readings that have not appeared in the foregoing chapters of Part Two are recorded here. Note that two of these characters (嚴 and 伍) have been assigned "official" readings for use in names.

藝		ゲイ		2352
R-3183	文藝	ブンゲイ	the literary arts	
	藝	わざ	skill; performance	

嘔		オウ		2999
R-3184	嘔吐	オウト	nausea	
	嘔く	はく	to spit up	

壽		ジュ・シュウ		2995
R-3185	長壽	チョウジュ	longevity	
	壽	ことぶき	felicitations	

國		コク		2988
R-3186	國家	コッカ	nation; state	
	國	くに	country	

嶋		トウ		2976
R-3187	列嶋	レットウ	archipelago	
	嶋	しま	island	

薗		エン		2974
R-3188	公薗	コウエン	public park	
	薗	その	park; garden	

龍 R-3189		リュウ・リョウ	2981
	龍頭蛇尾 龍安寺	リュウトウダビ リョウアンジ	good start, bad finish; anticlimax Temple of the Reclining Dragon (famous for its rock garden)

檜 R-3190			2964
	→ see FRAME R-2333		

燈 R-3191		トウ	2972
	燈台 燈 燈す 燈	トウダイ あかり ともす ひ	lighthouse bright light set alight torch; fire

嶽 R-3192		ガク	2987
	山嶽 嶽	サンガク たけ	mountains and peaks peak; point

巖 R-3193		ガン	2978
	溶巖 巖 巖 巖 巖	ヨウガン いわ いわお みち みね	molten lava rock; used in names used in names used in names used in names

什 R-3194		ジュウ・ジュッ	2968
	伍什 什点	ゴジュウ ジュッテン	fifty ten points

伍 R-3195		ゴ	2967
	伍什 伍	ゴジュウ くみ	fifty squadron; used for names

峯 R-3196		ホウ		2977
	峯頂 峯	ホウチョウ みね	top of a peak mountain summit	
舘 R-3197		カン		2980
	図書舘 舘	トショカン やかた	library manor	
慾 R-3198		ヨク		2984
	慾望 慾する 慾しい	ヨクボウ ほっする ほしい	craving; appetite to desire welcome; wished for	
淵 R-3199		エン		2966
	➔ see FRAME R-2952			
埜 R-3200		ヤ		2979
	埜心 埜	ヤシン の	wild; undomesticated field	
亙 R-3201		コウ		2985
	亙り 亙る	わたり わたる	crossing to cross over	

CHAPTER 14

Supplementary Kanji

THIS FINAL chapter is meant to encourage you to expand your proficiency beyond the range of 3,000. The 7 characters given here to get you going include the last 5 kanji from the Ministry of Education's official list of kanji (3001–3005) and 2 kanji that fell between the cracks of the selection process, but which you will find useful (3006–3007). Room has been left for you to add kanji of your own.

Only basic information has been provided in the first 7 frames, in a simplified layout different from the rest of the book. Each of the kanji has been assigned a key word, but no primitive elements or reading (R-) number. The information in the first 7 frames has also been incorporated into the Indexes.

亨 3001	go smoothly とおる・あきら・すすむ・ ちか・とし・みち・ゆき	[7] readings used in names	コウ・キョウ
侑 3002	condone すすむ・たす	[8] readings used in names	ユウ・ユ
梧 3003	parasol tree あおぎり	[11] Chinese parasol tree	ゴ
欽 3004	circumspect こく・ただ・ひとし・まこと	[12] readings used in names	キン
熙 3005	cheer かわく・てる・ひろ・ひろし・よし	[15] readings used in names	キ
而 3006	and then 形而上学　けいじじょうがく	[6] metaphysics	ジ

亭 3007	mandate	[7]	ヅイ・ジョウ
	掟　　おきて	commandment; mandate	
3008			
3009			
3010			
3011			
3012			
3013			
3014			
3015			

3016	
3017	
3018	
3019	
3020	
3021	
3022	
3023	
3024	

3025	
3026	
3027	
3028	
3029	
3030	
3031	
3032	
3033	

3034	
3035	
3036	
3037	
3038	
3039	
3040	
3041	
3042	

3043	
3044	
3045	
3046	
3047	
3048	
3049	
3050	

Indexes

INDEX I
Hand-Drawn Characters

The following Index includes all the kanji presented in Part One, in the order of their appearance. They are printed in one of the typical hand-drawn type styles to indicate proper form for drawing kanji by hand with a pen or pencil—the same form used in this book to show proper stroke order.

此	柴	砦	些	髭	璃	禽	檎	憐	燐
2043	2044	2045	2046	2047	2048	2049	2050	2051	2052
麟	鱗	奄	庵	掩	俺	悛	駿	峻	竣
2053	2054	2055	2056	2057	2058	2059	2060	2061	2062
臼	舅	鼠	鑿	毀	艘	犀	皐	脊	畷
2063	2064	2065	2066	2067	2068	2069	2070	2071	2072
綴	爾	璽	鎧	凱	妖	沃	呑	韮	籤
2073	2074	2075	2076	2077	2078	2079	2080	2081	2082
懺	芻	雛	趨	尤	稽	厖	采	或	斬
2083	2084	2085	2086	2087	2088	2089	2090	2091	2092
兎	也	尭	巴	甫	疋	董	曼	巾	云
2093	2094	2095	2096	2097	2098	2099	2100	2101	2102
卜	喬	莫	倭	俠	倦	佼	俄	佃	伶
2103	2104	2105	2106	2107	2108	2109	2110	2111	2112
仔	仇	伽	僅	僻	儲	倖	僑	侶	伎
2113	2114	2115	2116	2117	2118	2119	2120	2121	2122

侃	俱	侭	佑	俣	傭	偲	脩	倅	做
2123	2124	2125	2126	2127	2128	2129	2130	2131	2132
凄	冴	凋	凌	冶	凛	凧	凪	夙	鳳
2133	2134	2135	2136	2137	2138	2139	2140	2141	2142
劉	刹	剥	剃	匂	勾	厭	雁	贋	厨
2143	2144	2145	2146	2147	2148	2149	2150	2151	2152
仄	哨	嘲	咎	囁	喋	咽	嘩	噂	咳
2153	2154	2155	2156	2157	2158	2159	2160	2161	2162
喧	喉	唾	叩	嘘	啄	呪	吠	吊	噛
2163	2164	2165	2166	2167	2168	2169	2170	2171	2172
叶	吻	吃	噺	噌	唄	叱	邑	呆	喰
2173	2174	2175	2176	2177	2178	2179	2180	2181	2182
埴	坤	堆	壕	垢	坦	埠	填	堰	堵
2183	2184	2185	2186	2187	2188	2189	2190	2191	2192
嬰	姦	妬	婢	婉	娼	妓	娃	姪	嫉
2193	2194	2195	2196	2197	2198	2199	2200	2201	2202
嬬	姥	姑	姐	嬉	孕	孜	宥	寓	宏
2203	2204	2205	2206	2207	2208	2209	2210	2211	2212
牢	塞	宋	宍	屠	屁	屑	尻	屢	屍
2213	2214	2215	2216	2217	2218	2219	2220	2221	2222
屏	嵩	峻	峨	崖	嶺	嵌	嵯	帖	幡
2223	2224	2225	2226	2227	2228	2229	2230	2231	2232
幟	庖	廓	庇	鷹	庄	廟	彊	弥	弛
2233	2234	2235	2236	2237	2238	2239	2240	2241	2242

粥	挽	撞	扮	掠	挨	捆	捺	捻	搔
2243	2244	2245	2246	2247	2248	2249	2250	2251	2252
撰	拭	揃	捌	攪	摺	按	捉	拶	播
2253	2254	2255	2256	2257	2258	2259	2260	2261	2262
揖	托	捧	撚	挺	擾	挾	撫	撒	擢
2263	2264	2265	2266	2267	2268	2269	2270	2271	2272
捷	抉	怯	惟	惣	怜	怜	憧	恰	恢
2273	2274	2275	2276	2277	2278	2279	2280	2281	2282
悌	湧	澪	洸	滉	漱	洲	洵	滲	洒
2283	2284	2285	2286	2287	2288	2289	2290	2291	2292
沐	泪	渾	沙	洸	淫	梁	澱	氾	洛
2293	2294	2295	2296	2297	2298	2299	2300	2301	2302
汝	漉	瀨	濠	澆	溺	湊	淋	浩	汀
2303	2304	2305	2306	2307	2308	2309	2310	2311	2312
鴻	潅	溢	汰	湛	淳	潰	渥	灘	汲
2313	2314	2315	2316	2317	2318	2319	2320	2321	2322
瀞	溜	渕	沌	汎	濾	濡	淀	涅	釜
2323	2324	2325	2326	2327	2328	2329	2330	2331	2332
斧	爺	猾	猥	狡	狸	狼	狽	狗	狐
2333	2334	2335	2336	2337	2338	2339	2340	2341	2342
狛	狙	獅	狒	莨	茉	莉	苺	萩	藝
2343	2344	2345	2346	2347	2348	2349	2350	2351	2352
薤	蓑	萎	苔	蕩	蔽	蔓	蓮	芙	蓉
2353	2354	2355	2356	2357	2358	2359	2360	2361	2362

蘭	芦	薯	菖	蕉	芯	蕎	蕗	藍	茄
2363	2364	2365	2366	2367	2368	2369	2370	2371	2372
苟	蔭	蓬	芥	萌	葡	途	蘇	蕃	苓
2373	2374	2375	2376	2377	2378	2379	2380	2381	2382
菰	蒙	茅	芭	苅	蓋	葱	蔑	葵	茸
2383	2384	2385	2386	2387	2388	2389	2390	2391	2392
蕊	茸	蒔	芹	苫	葛	蒼	藁	蕪	藷
2393	2394	2395	2396	2397	2398	2399	2400	2401	2402
薮	蒜	蕨	蔚	茜	莞	蒐	菅	葦	迪
2403	2404	2405	2406	2407	2408	2409	2410	2411	2412
辿	這	迂	遁	逢	遥	遼	逼	迄	遜
2413	2414	2415	2416	2417	2418	2419	2420	2421	2422
逗	郁	鄭	隙	隈	憑	惹	悉	忽	惣
2423	2424	2425	2426	2427	2428	2429	2430	2431	2432
愈	恕	昴	晋	曖	晟	暈	暉	旱	晏
2433	2434	2435	2436	2437	2438	2439	2440	2441	2442
晨	晒	昧	晃	曝	曙	昂	旺	昏	晦
2443	2444	2445	2446	2447	2448	2449	2450	2451	2452
腎	股	膿	腑	胱	胚	肛	臆	膝	脆
2453	2454	2455	2456	2457	2458	2459	2460	2461	2462
肋	肘	腔	腺	腫	膳	肱	胡	楓	枕
2463	2464	2465	2466	2467	2468	2469	2470	2471	2472
楊	椋	榛	櫛	槌	樵	梯	椅	柿	柑
2473	2474	2475	2476	2477	2478	2479	2480	2481	2482

桁	杭	柊	柚	椀	栂	柾	榊	樫	槙
2483	2484	2485	2486	2487	2488	2489	2490	2491	2492
楢	橘	桧	棲	栖	梗	桔	杜	杷	梶
2493	2494	2495	2496	2497	2498	2499	2500	2501	2502
杵	杖	椎	樽	柵	櫓	橿	杓	李	棉
2503	2504	2505	2506	2507	2508	2509	2510	2511	2512
楯	榎	樺	槍	柘	梱	枇	樋	橇	槃
2513	2514	2515	2516	2517	2518	2519	2520	2521	2522
栞	椰	檀	樗	槻	椙	彬	桶	楕	櫟
2523	2524	2525	2526	2527	2528	2529	2530	2531	2532
毯	燿	燎	炬	焚	灸	燭	煽	煤	煉
2533	2534	2535	2536	2537	2538	2539	2540	2541	2542
燦	灼	烙	焔	熔	煎	烹	牽	牝	牡
2543	2544	2545	2546	2547	2548	2549	2550	2551	2552
瑶	琳	瑠	斑	琉	弄	瑳	琢	珊	瑚
2553	2554	2555	2556	2557	2558	2559	2560	2561	2562
瑞	珪	玖	瑛	玩	玲	畏	畢	畦	痒
2563	2564	2565	2566	2567	2568	2569	2570	2571	2572
痰	疹	痔	癌	痩	痕	痺	眸	眩	瞭
2573	2574	2575	2576	2577	2578	2579	2580	2581	2582
眉	雉	矩	磐	碇	碧	硯	砥	碗	碍
2583	2584	2585	2586	2587	2588	2589	2590	2591	2592
碩	磯	砺	碓	禦	祷	祐	祇	祢	禄
2593	2594	2595	2596	2597	2598	2599	2600	2601	2602

禎	秤	黍	禿	稔	稗	穰	稜	稀	穆
2603	2604	2605	2606	2607	2608	2609	2610	2611	2612

窺	窄	窟	穿	竈	竪	颯	站	靖	妾
2613	2614	2615	2616	2617	2618	2619	2620	2621	2622

衿	裾	袷	袴	襖	笙	筏	簾	簞	竿
2623	2624	2625	2626	2627	2628	2629	2630	2631	2632

篦	箔	筍	箭	筑	篭	篠	箸	簒	竺
2633	2634	2635	2636	2637	2638	2639	2640	2641	2642

箕	笈	篇	筈	簸	粕	糟	糊	籾	糠
2643	2644	2645	2646	2647	2648	2649	2650	2651	2652

糞	粟	繋	綸	絨	絆	緋	綜	紐	紘
2653	2654	2655	2656	2657	2658	2659	2660	2661	2662

纏	絢	繍	紬	綺	綾	絃	綻	縞	綬
2663	2664	2665	2666	2667	2668	2669	2670	2671	2672

紗	舵	舷	聯	聡	聘	耽	耶	蚤	蟹
2673	2674	2675	2676	2677	2678	2679	2680	2681	2682

蛋	蟄	蠅	蟻	蜂	蠟	蝦	蛸	螺	蝉
2683	2684	2685	2686	2687	2688	2689	2690	2691	2692

蛙	蛾	蛤	蛭	蛎	罪	罵	袈	裟	戴
2693	2694	2695	2696	2697	2698	2699	2700	2701	2702

截	哉	詢	諄	讐	諫	謎	諒	讃	誰
2703	2704	2705	2706	2707	2708	2709	2710	2711	2712

訊	訣	詣	諦	詮	詫	誼	謬	詫	諏
2713	2714	2715	2716	2717	2718	2719	2720	2721	2722

諺	誹	謂	諜	註	譬	轟	輔	輻	輯
2723	2724	2725	2726	2727	2728	2729	2730	2731	2732
貌	豹	賤	貼	貰	賂	賑	躓	蹄	蹴
2733	2734	2735	2736	2737	2738	2739	2740	2741	2742
蹟	跨	跪	醬	醍	酎	醐	醒	醇	麺
2743	2744	2745	2746	2747	2748	2749	2750	2751	2752
麴	釦	銚	鋤	鍋	鏑	鋸	錐	鍵	鍬
2753	2754	2755	2756	2757	2758	2759	2760	2761	2762
鋲	錫	錨	釘	鑢	鋒	鎚	鉦	錆	鍾
2763	2764	2765	2766	2767	2768	2769	2770	2771	2772
鋏	閃	悶	閤	闇	雫	霞	翰	幹	鞍
2773	2774	2775	2776	2777	2778	2779	2780	2781	2782
鞭	鞘	鞄	靭	鞠	頓	顛	穎	頃	頬
2783	2784	2785	2786	2787	2788	2789	2790	2791	2792
頗	頌	顎	頚	餌	餐	饗	蝕	飴	餅
2793	2794	2795	2796	2797	2798	2799	2800	2801	2802
駕	驊	馳	騙	馴	駁	駈	驢	鰻	鯛
2803	2804	2805	2806	2807	2808	2809	2810	2811	2812
鰯	鱒	鮭	鮪	鮎	鯵	鱈	鯖	鮫	鰹
2813	2814	2815	2816	2817	2818	2819	2820	2821	2822
鰍	鰐	鮒	鮨	鰭	鴎	鵬	鸚	鵡	鵜
2823	2824	2825	2826	2827	2828	2829	2830	2831	2832
鷺	鷲	鴨	鳶	梟	塵	麓	麒	冥	瞑
2833	2834	2835	2836	2837	2838	2839	2840	2841	2842

暝	坐	挫	朔	遡	曳	洩	彗	慧	嘉
2843	2844	2845	2846	2847	2848	2849	2850	2851	2852
兒	兜	爽	欝	劫	勃	歉	輿	巽	歪
2853	2854	2855	2856	2857	2858	2859	2860	2861	2862
翠	黛	鼎	鹵	鹼	虔	燕	嘗	殆	孟
2863	2864	2865	2866	2867	2868	2869	2870	2871	2872
牌	骸	覘	彪	秦	雀	隼	耀	夷	戚
2873	2874	2875	2876	2877	2878	2879	2880	2881	2882
囊	丼	暢	廻	畿	欣	毅	斯	匙	匡
2883	2884	2885	2886	2887	2888	2889	2890	2891	2892
肇	磨	叢	肴	斐	卿	甌	於	套	叛
2893	2894	2895	2896	2897	2898	2899	2900	2901	2902
尖	壺	叡	酉	鴬	赫	臥	甥	瓢	琵
2903	2904	2905	2906	2907	2908	2909	2910	2911	2912
琶	叉	舜	畠	拳	圍	丞	亮	胤	疏
2913	2914	2915	2916	2917	2918	2919	2920	2921	2922
膏	魁	馨	牒	瞥	阜	皐	巫	敦	奎
2923	2924	2925	2926	2927	2928	2929	2930	2931	2932
翔	皓	黎	赳	已	棘	聚	甦	剪	躬
2933	2934	2935	2936	2937	2938	2939	2940	2941	2942
夥	軒	崇	粁	糎	粍	噸	哩	浬	吋
2943	2944	2945	2946	2947	2948	2949	2950	2951	2952
呎	梵	陀	薩	菩	啞	迦	那	牟	珈
2953	2954	2955	2956	2957	2958	2959	2960	2961	2962

琲	檜	彎	淵	伍	什	萬	邁	逞	燈
2963	2964	2965	2966	2967	2968	2969	2970	2971	2972
裡	薗	鋪	嶋	峯	巖	埜	舘	龍	寵
2973	2974	2975	2976	2977	2978	2979	2980	2981	2982
聳	慫	互	躯	嶽	國	脛	勁	箋	祀
2983	2984	2985	2986	2987	2988	2989	2990	2991	2992
祓	蹢	壽	躊	彙	饅	嘔	鼇		
2993	2994	2995	2996	2997	2998	2999	3000		

INDEX II

Primitive Elements

This Index is a cumulative listing of all the primitive elements and signal primitives introduced in VOLS. 1 to 3, arranged according to the number of strokes. Primitive elements assigned meanings are referenced to the volume and page number on which they appear. Signal primitives are referenced to the frame numbers of VOLS. 2 and 3.

INDEX III

Kanji in Stroke Order

Index III includes all the kanji covered in VOLS. 1, 2, and 3, arranged according to number of strokes and radical. The numbers refer to the frame in which the kanji was first introduced. To locate the reading frame for kanji from VOL. 1, consult Index V in VOL. 2. Frames in Part One and Part Three of this volume are already cross-referenced to Part Two.

	跳	1284
	路	1282
車	較	1277
	載	359
辛	辞	1497
辰	農	2014
辶	逼	2420
	遍	1824
	違	1644
	遠	402
	遣	1773
	遡	2847
	遜	2422
酉	酬	1432
	酪	1433
金	鉛	794
	鉱	741
	鉦	2770
	鉄	846
	鉢	271
	鈴	1406
	隔	1312
	隙	2426
	雅	1907
	雉	2584
雨	電	535
	雷	425
	零	1402
革	靴	1894
頁	頑	61
	頌	2794
	頓	2788
	頒	783
	預	1595
	飴	2801
	飼	1866
	飾	1477
	飽	1480
	馴	2807
	馳	2805
鳥	鳩	1946
	鼎	2865

	鼓	1444
	鼠	2065

14画

	僑	2120
亻	像	1977
	僕	1794
	僚	1707
	厭	2149
口	嘔	2999
	嘉	2852
	噌	2177
	嘗	2870
土	境	484
	塾	309
	塵	2838
	増	502
	墨	175
	夥	2943
大	奪	566
	嫡	440
	寡	617
	察	1103
	寧	834
	壽	2995
尸	層	1065
	嶋	2976
	廓	2235
	彰	1715
彳	徴	887
	徳	885
	態	2005
	慕	633
	慣	627
	憎	626
	慢	829
	截	2703
	摺	2258
	摘	657
	幹	2781
	旗	1764
	暢	2885

日	暮	232
	暝	2843
	暦	213
	膏	2923
	膜	233
木	榎	2514
	樺	2515
	概	1482
	構	1818
	榛	2475
	槍	2516
	槙	2492
	槃	2522
	模	229
	様	933
	樋	2520
	歌	469
止	歴	376
	演	2007
	潅	2314
	漁	172
	漬	1545
	漆	932
	滲	2291
	漸	1135
	漱	2288
	漕	1175
	滴	442
	漂	1607
	漫	830
	漏	1068
	漉	2304
	煽	2540
	熔	2547
	熊	2003
	爾	2074
	獄	338
	瑳	2559
	瑠	2555
疒	疑	1410
	磁	1390
	碩	2593

	碑	1512
	碧	2588
禾	穀	917
	種	1679
	稲	910
穴	窪	1323
立	竪	2618
	端	1167
竹	箇	2029
	管	1273
	箕	2643
	算	946
	箋	2991
	箔	2634
	箆	2633
	箸	2640
米	精	1535
糸	維	1341
	綺	2667
	綱	1963
	綬	2672
	緒	1344
	綜	2660
	総	1366
	綻	2670
	綴	2073
	緋	2659
	綿	1367
	網	1373
	綾	2668
	緑	1371
	綸	2656
	練	1343
	辜	2929
	罰	833
	翠	2863
	聚	2939
	聡	2677
	聞	1626
	肇	2893
肉	腐	1023
廾	蔭	2374

	蔚	2406
	蔦	1945
	蔑	2390
	蔓	2359
	蜜	776
	蝋	2688
	蝕	2800
	裳	800
	製	419
	複	465
言	語	347
	誤	1899
	誌	601
	誓	1133
	説	499
	読	348
	認	598
	誘	916
豕	豪	543
	貌	2733
	賑	2739
	赫	2908
足	踊	1409
	輔	2730
辶	遮	1192
	遭	1174
	適	441
酉	酵	1430
	酷	1431
	酸	1437
金	銀	1459
	銃	762
	銭	368
	銑	270
	銚	2755
	銅	272
	銘	275
門	閣	1624
	関	2017
	閤	2776
	閥	1619
	隠	1313

Chinese Readings

This Index includes all the Chinese readings treated in VOLS. 2 and 3, arranged in standard dictionary order, and the numbers of each frame in which a particular reading is introduced.

【ア】			慰	R-359	郁	R-3008	有	R-2112	
ア	亜	R-1818	意	R-856	イチ 一	R-965	羽	R-2043	
	唖	R-2415	医	R-935	壱	R-973	迂	R-2393	
	蛙	R-2752	夷	R-2990	イツ 逸	R-1868	胡	R-2605	
	阿	R-2235	已	R-3029	一	R-966	ウツ 蔚	R-2559	
アイ	哀	R-1095	彙	R-3084	溢	R-2953	欝	R-2936	
	挨	R-3060	囲	R-1131	イン 員	R-839	ウン 運	R-1067	
	曖	R-2436	違	R-1221	韻	R-840	雲	R-1843	
	愛	R-1096	偉	R-1222	因	R-905	暈	R-2758	
	娃	R-2753	緯	R-1223	咽	R-2598	云	R-2848	
アク	悪	R-1704	葦	R-2661	姻	R-906			
	握	R-1873	衣	R-1566	韻	R-1299	**【エ】**		
	渥	R-2547	位	R-1578	音	R-1300	エ	衣	R-23
アツ	圧	R-538	依	R-1627	院	R-1158		恵	R-31
	斡	R-2803	惟	R-2787	印	R-1731		会	R-384
アン	安	R-52	維	R-1630	引	R-1806		絵	R-385
	按	R-2289	易	R-1705	飯	R-1841		依	R-2226
	案	R-315	椅	R-2542	淫	R-2850		回	R-2232
	晏	R-2291	委	R-1706	胤	R-2989		慧	R-2893
	暗	R-1301	萎	R-2533	蔭	R-2404	エイ	永	R-194
	行	R-2238	移	R-1775	陰	R-1931		泳	R-195
	鞍	R-2290	胃	R-1809	隠	R-2213		詠	R-196
	庵	R-2582	謂	R-2414	允	R-2161		英	R-827
	闇	R-2714	遺	R-1813			瑛	R-2434	
			異	R-1814	**【ウ】**		映	R-828	
【イ】			畏	R-2588	ウ	宇	R-30	営	R-1026
イ	以	R-11	威	R-1870	雨	R-1545	衛	R-1224
	為	R-26	唯	R-2164	右	R-1754	鋭	R-1394
	伊	R-33	イキ 域	R-551	佑	R-2648	影	R-1595
	尉	R-358	イク 育	R-1141	烏	R-1929	栄	R-1699

	除	R-1510		酒	R-2801		需	R-366		酋	R-2938
	児	R-1571		柘	R-3028		儒	R-367		壽	R-3185
	次	R-1619		砂	R-2153		嬬	R-2305	ジュウ	充	R-97
	示	R-1744		紗	R-2853		濡	R-2306		銃	R-918
	似	R-1784		這	R-3064		樹	R-1613		従	R-368
	耳	R-1839	ジャ	邪	R-787		寿	R-1859		縦	R-369
	餌	R-2811	シャク	尺	R-1159		壽	R-3185		十	R-971
	仕	R-2262		昔	R-1494		就	R-2086		什	R-3194
シキ	識	R-932		借	R-1498		呪	R-2930		汁	R-2027
	織	R-934		釈	R-1572		聚	R-3038		住	R-995
	色	R-1130		酌	R-1925	シュウ	州	R-257		柔	R-1007
	式	R-1587		石	R-2018		洲	R-258		重	R-1625
ジキ	直	R-1325		赤	R-2113		酬	R-259		獣	R-1879
	食	R-2045		勺	R-2197		秋	R-482		渋	R-1975
ジク	竺	R-2847		杓	R-2815		愁	R-483		拾	R-2081
	軸	R-552		灼	R-2816		萩	R-2308		絨	R-2851
シチ	七	R-968		爵	R-2218		鍬	R-2307		聚	R-3038
	質	R-1904		錫	R-2957		週	R-1018	シュク	宿	R-492
シツ	室	R-1025	ジャク	寂	R-1298		柊	R-2875		縮	R-493
	質	R-1037		弱	R-1782		終	R-1053		祝	R-1279
	失	R-1061		若	R-1962		祝	R-1279		叔	R-1295
	叱	R-2924		惹	R-2747		袖	R-1350		淑	R-1296
	湿	R-1736		着	R-2131		周	R-1533		粛	R-2085
	執	R-1745		雀	R-2858		週	R-1534		夙	R-2946
	漆	R-1907	シュ	朱	R-182		収	R-1552	ジュク	塾	R-370
	膝	R-2430		殊	R-183		集	R-1576		熟	R-371
	疾	R-1923		珠	R-184		讐	R-2979	シュツ	出	R-571
	嫉	R-2429		守	R-516		宗	R-1588	ジュツ	什	R-3194
	悉	R-2566		狩	R-517		就	R-1689	ジュツ	述	R-376
	櫛	R-2942		主	R-997		蹴	R-2362		術	R-377
ジッ	十	R-1156		手	R-1052		鷲	R-2363	シュン	隼	R-2426
ジツ	日	R-1574		主	R-1335		衆	R-1749		洵	R-2580
	実	R-1629		取	R-1466		襲	R-1763		詢	R-2579
シャ	叉	R-2971		諏	R-3071		修	R-1768		舜	R-2440
	射	R-506		趣	R-1467		脩	R-2852		瞬	R-1585
	謝	R-507		首	R-1565		囚	R-1778		春	R-1894
	舎	R-911		種	R-1658		拾	R-1813		俊	R-2074
	捨	R-912		腫	R-2884		秀	R-1868		峻	R-2500
	者	R-936		酒	R-1661		蒐	R-2829		悛	R-2501
	社	R-941		手	R-1573		醜	R-1976		竣	R-2502
	車	R-955		修	R-2234		執	R-2131		駿	R-2503
	写	R-1028		衆	R-2239		揖	R-2591	ジュン	旬	R-372
	煮	R-1361		撞	R-2318		葺	R-2589		洵	R-2580
	遮	R-1963	ジュ	受	R-364		輯	R-2590		殉	R-373
	赦	R-2004		授	R-365		舟	R-2185		詢	R-2579
	斜	R-2066		綬	R-2326		繍	R-2917		盾	R-374

	苔 R-2656	箪 R-2797	躓 R-3034	脹 R-68

苔 R-2656
体 R-1084
大 R-1073
太 R-1150
汰 R-2433
黛 R-2278
堆 R-2783
退 R-1401
逮 R-1679
態 R-1690
隊 R-1773
泰 R-1818
耐 R-1905
替 R-2137
戴 R-2697
ダイ 大 R-960
題 R-1038
醍 R-2840
台 R-1088
代 R-1099
第 R-1116
弟 R-1417
内 R-2007
タク 宅 R-458
托 R-2337
託 R-459
卓 R-1639
拓 R-1644
択 R-1996
沢 R-1062
度 R-2111
濯 R-2208
啄 R-2929
琢 R-2906
ダク 諾 R-1760
濁 R-1889
タツ 達 R-572
ダツ 脱 R-1395
奪 R-1906
タン 旦 R-715
胆 R-716
担 R-717
坦 R-2554
壇 R-718
檀 R-2425
単 R-1000

箪 R-2797
誕 R-1063
反 R-1234
短 R-1448
炭 R-1735
探 R-1765
嘆 R-1832
歎 R-2796
灘 R-2805
蛋 R-2950
鍛 R-1880
淡 R-1887
痰 R-2781
端 R-1967
丹 R-2216
綻 R-2669
耽 R-2916
湛 R-3017
站 R-3037
ダン 男 R-950
団 R-957
談 R-994
段 R-1001
断 R-1581
暖 R-1733
弾 R-1861
壇 R-2148
檀 R-2425

【チ】
チ 知 R-9
痴 R-189
智 R-190
地 R-956
池 R-1288
弛 R-2771
馳 R-2772
治 R-1267
値 R-1321
置 R-1322
雉 R-2782
稚 R-1637
遅 R-1886
致 R-1997
恥 R-2005
質 R-2204

躓 R-3034
ヂ 地 R-1004
地 R-1287
チク 畜 R-326
蓄 R-327
筑 R-2410
築 R-1617
竹 R-2036
逐 R-2061
チツ 秩 R-1379
窒 R-2065
蟄 R-3030
チャ 茶 R-543
チャク 着 R-1671
嫡 R-2180
チュウ 中 R-57
忠 R-58
沖 R-59
仲 R-60
昼 R-719
注 R-1128
注 R-1331
柱 R-1332
駐 R-1333
註 R-1334
宙 R-1347
抽 R-1448
紬 R-2777
紐 R-2455
虫 R-2022
厨 R-2866
肘 R-2980
酎 R-2901
躊 R-3053
鋳 R-2073
衷 R-2214
チョ 著 R-1365
躇 R-2737
儲 R-2738
猪 R-1366
緒 R-1367
貯 R-1462
樗 R-3006
チョウ 長 R-65
張 R-66
帳 R-67

脹 R-68
徴 R-328
懲 R-329
朝 R-330
嘲 R-2578
潮 R-331
超 R-684
兆 R-1168
跳 R-1169
挑 R-1170
眺 R-1171
銚 R-2645
腸 R-1372
暢 R-2732
澄 R-1447
丁 R-1458
挺 R-2276
町 R-1459
頂 R-1460
庁 R-1461
凋 R-2766
調 R-1531
彫 R-1532
鯛 R-2767
聴 R-1590
重 R-1720
鳥 R-1838
弔 R-1874
喋 R-2506
牒 R-2507
諜 R-2508
蝶 R-1885
釣 R-2189
帖 R-2878
吊 R-3056
貼 R-2877
籠 R-2922
肇 R-3005
チョク 直 R-1325
勅 R-1498
捗 R-2996
チン 賃 R-904
鎮 R-925
陳 R-1330
沈 R-1727
枕 R-3021

狼 R-2603		糧 R-2105	麓 R-2371		猥 R-2587
牢 R-2927		蝋 R-2943	ロン 論 R-901		隈 R-2586
労 R-1112		聾 R-2869		ワク 惑 R-1550	
弄 R-2951	ロク	六 R-971	【ワ】	ワン 椀 R-2633	
老 R-1146		肋 R-2981	ワ 和 R-12		碗 R-2634
楼 R-1876		録 R-296	倭 R-2534		腕 R-783
漏 R-1911		緑 R-297	杷 R-2765		湾 R-1102
稜 R-2352		禄 R-2340	話 R-947		
露 R-2079		鹿 R-2229	ワイ 歪 R-2897		
篭 R-2868		漉 R-2370	賄 R-573		

Japanese Readings

This Index includes only the Japanese readings established as standard for the "General-Use Kanji." Any characters treated in this book and VOL. 1 that fall outside that list are given only with their most common readings. The numbers refer to the frames in VOL. 1 and Part One of the present volume.

【い】

たまや	廟	2239
たまり	溜	2324
だまる	黙る	240
たまわる	賜る	1052
たみ	民	1834
たむろ	屯	2033
ため	為	1918f
ためす	試す	354
	験す	1980
ためらう	躊う	2994
ためる	矯める	1221
	溜める	2324
	貯る	194
たもつ	保つ	997
たやす	絶やす	1754
たより	便り	991
たよる	頼る	1665
たら	鱈	2819
たらい	盤	2522
	盤	1872
たらす	垂らす	1582
たりる	足りる	1279
たる	足る	1279
	樽	2506
たるむ	弛む	2242
たれ	誰	2712
だれ	誰	2712
たれる	垂れる	1582
たわむれる	戯れる	1994
たわら	俵	1547

【ち】

ち	千	40
	血	1448
	乳	729
	茅	2385
ちいさい	小さい	105
	繊さい	1790
ちえ	智	1224
ちか	哉	2704
	爾	2074
	睦	1514
ちかい	近い	1129
ちかう	誓う	1133
	盟う	1450
ちがう	違う	1644

ちがえる	違える	1644
ちかづく	近づく	1129
ちがや	茅	2385
ちから	力	858
ちぎる	契る	1549
ちち	父	1274
	乳	729
ちちざけ	酪	1433
ちぢまる	縮まる	1336
ちぢむ	縮む	1336
ちぢめる	縮める	1336
ちぢらす	縮らす	1336
ちぢれる	縮れる	1336
ちなむ	因む	583
ちらかす	散らかす	1189
ちらかる	散らかる	1189
ちらす	散らす	1189
ちり	塵	2838
ちる	散る	1189

【つ】

つ	津	328
ついえる	費える	1238
	潰える	2319
ついたち	朔	2846
ついで	序で	1594
	叙で	1660
	第	1239
ついに	遂に	540
	畢に	2570
	了に	97
ついばむ	啄む	2168
ついやす	費やす	1238
つえ	杖	2504
つか	塚	1039
	杷	2501
つが	栂	2488
つがい	番い	1909
つかう	使う	990
	遣う	1773
つかえる	仕える	960
つかさ	司	1863
	吏	693
	官	1271
	宰	1499
	曹	1173

なんじ	汝	2303
	而	3006
	爾	2074
なんぞ	那	2960
	胡	2470

【に】

に	荷	1013
	丹	2038
にい	新	1502
にえ	牲	1559
にえる	煮える	1257
におい	匂い	2147
	臭い	122
におう	匂う	2147
	臭う	122
にがい	苦い	225
にがす	逃がす	283
にがる	苦る	225
にぎやか	賑やか	2739
にぎる	握る	1059
にぎわい	賑わい	2739
にくい	憎い	626
にくしみ	憎しみ	626
にくむ	憎む	626
にくらしい	憎らしい	626
にげる	逃げる	283
にごす	濁す	835
にごる	濁る	835
	渾る	2295
にし	西	1602
	螺	2691
にじ	虹	520
にしき	錦	411
にじむ	滲む	2291
にじゅう	廿	1190
にせ	偽	1919
	贋	2151
にせる	肖せる	114
になう	担う	668
にぶい	鈍い	1495
にぶる	鈍る	1495
にやす	煮やす	1257
にら	韮	2081
にる	似る	1029
	煮る	1257

にわ	烹る	2549
にわ	庭	590
にわか	俄	2110
にわとり	鶏	1947

【ぬ】

ぬいとり	繍	2665
ぬう	縫う	1563
ぬか	糠	2652
ぬかす	抜かす	705
ぬきんでる	擢でる	2272
	抜きんでる	705
ぬく	抜く	705
	挺く	2267
	抽く	1106
ぬぐ	脱ぐ	498
ぬぐう	拭う	2254
ぬける	抜ける	705
ぬげる	脱げる	498
ぬさ	幣	1040
ぬし	主	266
ぬすむ	盗む	1451
	窃む	1322
ぬた	饅	2998
ぬの	布	405
ぬま	沼	137
ぬる	塗る	1663
ぬれる	濡れる	2329

【ね】

ね	音	479
	根	1461
	子	95
	値	978
	嶺	2228
ねえ	姐	2206
ねがう	願う	135
	希う	1489
ねかす	寝かす	1150
ねぎ	葱	2389
ねぎらう	労う	860
ねこ	猫	244
ねじ	螺	2691
ねじる	捻る	2251
ねずみ	鼠	2065

ねたむ	嫉む	2202			延びる	392
	妬む	2195			展びる	1925
ねばる	粘る	921			暢びる	2885
ねむい	眠い	1835	のぶ	允		765
ねむる	眠る	1835		惣		2432
ねらう	狙う	2344		暢		2885
ねる	寝る	1150		寅		2006
	練る	1343		靖		2621
	煉る	2542		洵		2290
	錬る	2030		脩		2130
ねんごろ	懇ろ	1970	のべる	延べる		392
	諄ろ	2706		述べる		1524
ねんじる	念じる	1590		叙べる		1660
				宣べる		188
	【の】			展べる		1925
の	野	1596		陳べる		1301
	埜	2979		演べる		2007
	乃	686	のぼす	上す		49
	之	1214	のぼせる	上せる		49
のがす	逃す	283	のぼり	幟		2233
のがれる	逃れる	283	のぼる	上る		49
	逸れる	1973		昇る		43
	遁れる	2416		登る		1703
のき	軒	1652		騰る		1989
のぎ	秒	899	のみ	蚤		2681
のこぎり	鋸	2759		鑿		2066
のこす	残す	808	のむ	飲む		1474
	遺す	1772		呑む		2080
のこる	残る	808		喫む		1550
	遺る	1772	のり	矩		2585
のせる	乗せる	1585		糊		2650
	載せる	359		則		88
	駄せる	1986		刑		679
のぞき	覗き	2875		式		353
のぞく	除く	1658		典		1827
	覗く	2875		法		751
	窺く	2613		律		874
のぞむ	望む	489		儀		984
	臨む	854		範		1413
のち	後	1379		憲		1554
のど	咽	2159	のる	乗る		1585
	喉	2164		載る		359
ののしる	罵る	2699		駕る		2803
のばす	伸ばす	1118		宣る		188
	延ばす	392		搭る		646
のびる	伸びる	1118		騎る		1981

	賞める	796
	讃める	2711
ほら	洞	181
ほり	濠	2306
	堀	1062
ほる	彫る	1710
	掘る	1061
ほれる	惚れる	2277
ほろ	幌	410
ほろびる	亡びる	485
	滅びる	365
ほろぼす	滅ぼす	365

【ま】

ま	目	15
	真	75
	馬	1978
	間	1620
まい	舞	1774
まいなう	賂う	2738
	賄う	80
まいる	参る	1720
	詣る	2715
マイル	哩	2950
まう	舞う	1774
まえ	前	290
まがき	藩	1912
まかす	任す	1003
	負かす	63
まかせる	任せる	1003
まかなう	賄う	80
まがる	曲がる	1172
まき	牧	329
	巻	1207
	蒔	2395
	薪	1503
	槙	2492
まぎらす	紛らす	1358
まぎらわしい	紛らわしい	1358
まぎらわす	紛らわす	1358
まぎれる	紛れる	1358
まく	巻く	1207
	撒く	2271
	蒔く	2395
	播く	2262
まぐさ	芻	2084

まくら	枕	2472
まぐろ	鮪	2816
まける	負ける	63
まげる	曲げる	1172
まご	孫	1393
まごころ	忠	602
まこと	誠	363
	允	765
	亮	2920
	諒	2710
	洵	2290
	信	969
	真	75
	惇	2279
	款	1097
まことに	洵に	2290
	諒に	2710
まこも	菰	2383
まさ	正	379
	允	765
	匡	2892
	昌	25
	柾	2489
まさき	柾	2489
まさに	応に	607
	将に	731
	鼎に	2865
まさる	勝る	1209
	愈る	2433
	賢る	852
まざる	交ざる	1275
	混ざる	450
まじえる	交える	1275
まじない	呪	2169
まじる	交じる	1275
	混じる	450
	雑じる	562
	錯じる	1185
まじわる	交わる	1275
ます	升	42
	鱒	2814
	益す	1881
	増す	502
まず	先	248
まずい	拙い	769
まずしい	貧しい	782

やすい	安い	190
	易い	1051
	泰い	1570
	康い	1159
	賎い	2735
	寧い	834
	靖い	2621
やすし	欣	2888
	悌	2283
	靖	2621
やすまる	休まる	965
やすむ	休む	965
やすめる	休める	965
やすらか	晏らか	2442
やすんずる	靖ずる	2621
やせる	痩せる	2577
やつ	八つ	8
	奴	702
やっつ	八つ	8
やど	宿	995
やとう	雇う	1083
	傭う	2128
	賃う	1004
やどす	宿す	995
やどる	宿る	995
	舎る	316
やなぎ	柳	1421
	楊	2473
やに	脂	456
やぶ	薮	2403
やぶる	破る	806
やぶれる	破れる	806
	敗れる	331
	弊れる	1041
やま	山	768
やまい	病	1682
	疾	1686
やまと	倭	2106
やみ	闇	2777
やむ	病む	1682
	止む	370
	疾む	1686
やめる	辞める	1497
	已める	2937
やり	槍	2516
	鑓	2767

やる	遣る	1773
やわらか	柔らか	1226
	軟らか	470
やわらかい	柔らかい	1226
	軟らかい	470
やわらぐ	和らぐ	897
やわらげる	和らげる	897

【ゆ】

ゆ	湯	546
ゆう	夕	109
	結う	1351
ゆえ	故	333
ゆか	床	592
ゆがむ	歪む	2862
ゆき	雪	1143
	之	1214
ゆく	行く	873
	逝く	1132
	之く	1214
	往く	880
	征く	881
	適く	441
	邁く	2970
ゆげ	汽	1886
ゆさぶる	揺さぶる	1967
ゆず	柚	2486
ゆする	揺する	1967
ゆずる	譲る	1528
	禅る	1930
	遜る	2422
ゆたか	豊か	1443
	浩	2311
	穣	2609
	裕	793
ゆだねる	委ねる	913
ゆび	指	659
ゆみ	弓	1231
	弧	1878
ゆめ	夢	305
ゆらぐ	揺らぐ	1967
ゆる	揺る	1967
ゆるい	緩い	1952
ゆるぐ	揺るぐ	1967
ゆるす	許す	569
	宥す	2210

INDEX VI

Key Words and Primitive Meanings

Index VI contains a cumulative list of all the key words and primitive meanings used in VOLS. *1 and 3. The key words are listed with their respective kanji and frame number. Primitive meanings are listed in italics and are followed only by the number of the volume and page on which they are first introduced.*

I (one)	壱	457	accusation	訴	1139	again, or	又	696
II (two)	弐	355	accustomed	慣	627	age	齢	1403
			achievement	功	863	aged woman	姥	2204
A			acid	酸	1437	aggression	攻	330
a	或	2091	acknowledge	認	598	aglow	晟	2438
abacus		*1.307*	*acorn*		*1.326*	agony	悶	2775
abandon	棄	758	acquiesce	承	1901	agreement	肯	374
abbreviation	略	293	*acupuncturist*		*1.31*	agriculture	農	2014
abdomen	腹	464	add	加	867	aid	扶	839
abet	援	1951	addiction	耽	2679	aim at	狙	2344
abide by	遵	2031	address	宛	1417	air out	曝	2447
ability	能	2004	adhere	付	1000	alienate	疎	1668
abolish	廃	1706	adjusted	斉	1729	all	皆	449
abounding	浩	2311	adjutant	佑	2126	alliance	盟	1450
about that time	頃	2791	admirable	偉	1643	alligator	鰐	2824
above	上	49	admonish	警	336	allot	充	761
above-stated	該	1522	adore	崇	1101	almost	殆	2871
abrupt	俄	2110	adroit	巧	1241	alms	施	1045
abundant	裕	793	advance	進	561	*altar*		*1.264*
abuse	弊	1041	advise	諏	2722	alternate	迭	847
abyss [old]	淵	2966	*aerosol can*		*1.129*	amass	蓄	1385
abyss	渕	2325	affair	件	959	ambition	望	489
accept	受	735	affinity	縁	1372	ambrosial	馨	2925
accept humbly	戴	2702	affix	貼	2736	ancestor	祖	1779
accidentally	偶	1955	affixed	附	1303	ancestral shrine	祢	2601
accolade	頌	2794	afflicted	患	604	ancestral tablet	祐	2599
accompany	従	877	Africa	阿	1295	anchor	錨	2765
accomplished	達	552	again	再	1815	ancient harp	筑	2637
accumulate	累	1364